IF JESUS GAVE A
TED TALK

Eight **NEUROSCIENCE** principles the Master
Teacher used to persuade His audience

CHARLES STONE

FREILING
PUBLISHING

Table of Contents

1

Introduction

How I am taught shapes my brain as much as or more than what I am taught.[1]
—Tracey Tokuhama-Espinosa

They delicately cinched the form-fitted mask over her head as her five-year-old body lay motionless. We prayed for her and walked out of the room that was filled with hi-tech equipment. She showed more bravery than we did. As we exited, they closed a 13-inch-thick metal door behind us.

We asked them how long it would take.

They said, "Only a few minutes."

We then heard the slight whir begin behind the leaded walls as the cyclotron started. It sounded like the buzz from a transformer on top of a telephone pole, only louder.

In ten minutes, it was over … until the next day.

They slowly re-opened the massive door, and we walked in.

There she lay, motionless. The technician gingerly unscrewed the toggle bolts that held the mask in place. They removed it, and she sat up.

I asked, "Tiffany, did you feel anything?"

"No, Daddy," she replied. "I didn't feel a thing."

---

[1] Tracey Tokuhama-Espinosa, *Making Classrooms Better: 50 Practical Applications of Mind, Brain, and Education Science*, 1 edition (New York: W. W. Norton & Company, 2014), p. 86.

For the next six weeks, that became our routine five times a week.

Four years prior, doctors had discovered a brain tumor deep within our youngest daughter's brain. Three brain surgeries later, we found ourselves in Loma Linda, California, for hi-tech proton-beam radiotherapy to kill the remaining tumor in her brain.

Almost 30 years later, Tiffany is doing well, and we credit God's power and the treatment that killed the tumor.

What made this kind of treatment so effective was its delivery method. Over those six weeks, the doctors changed the beam's angle in her brain each time Tiffany received treatment. Maximum radiation was created where the beams intersected in the tumor. As they intersected at the tumor site, they slowly killed it while still protecting healthy brain tissue that received little radiation. It's called stereotactic radiation.

Great communicators actually use a similar concept when they speak, teach, preach, or train. They intersect potent communication principles which give their speeches, sermons, lessons, and training sessions great power. That's what this book is about.

* * *

The greatest communicator ever lived 2,000 years ago. He held no academic degrees, wrote no books, held no formal classes, never used a PowerPoint slide or an iPad, and taught and lived in an obscure corner of the world. As He taught, He felt equally at home with a simple villager as He did with a Roman governor, yet His message turned history upside down and has transformed billions of lives. He has been called "our only teacher," "the greatest of the greatest oral teachers," the "master teacher," and the "paragon of pedagogy."[2]

His name? Jesus of Nazareth.

His message? The Gospel—the Good News from God.

His medium to deliver His message? Oral communication.

His audience? From the rich to the poor, the ignorant to the learned, and intimate one-on-one conversations to sermons delivered to thousands.

His result? Christianity—the faith of billions.

Jesus masterfully intersected several communication principles which helped make His teaching so potent. The Gospel writers recorded it for us. They wrote over 50 times that He was called *teacher*. His listeners described His teaching as having authority. They noted over ten times that people were "amazed" at His teaching, and they recorded over 25 extended discourses.[3] They "hung on His words" (Luke 19:48), "listened with delight" (Mark 12:37), and crowded around Him to hear Him teach (Luke 5:1). He enthralled the crowds so well that sometimes they even forgot to eat (Mark 6:22-44). Crowds would often gather, not just to receive His miracles but to hear Him teach.[4]

And when the temple guards arrested Jesus before He was crucified, they remarked, "No one ever spoke the way this man does" (John 7:46). One study notes that Scripture gives

---

[2] David Naugle, "Information or Transformation? The Pedagogy of Jesus the Master Teacher and Its Implications," 2004, https://www3.dbu.edu/naugle/pdf/FridaySymposiumSp04/Pedagogy_of_Jesus.pdf, p. 9.

[3] Robert G. Delnay, *Teach As He Taught: How to Apply Jesus' Teaching Methods* (Chicago: Moody Pub, 1987).

[4] Robert H. Stein, *The Method and Message of Jesus' Teachings, Revised Edition*, Revised, Subsequent edition (Louisville, Ky: Westminster John Knox Press, 1994), p. 7.

42 names and titles for Jesus with teacher ranked as the fourth most often used title.[5]

Even the early church fathers such as Clement and Ignatius called Jesus "our only teacher," "our tutor," and an "educator."[6]

What about Jesus' communication and teaching elicited such comments and motivated so many to believe His message and follow Him? What made Him such a profound communicator? Did He use techniques that modern day speechmakers, teachers, preachers, and businesspeople can apply in their speeches, lessons, sermons, and training sessions?

I'm convinced He did. He inspired His learners with teachable moments. He guided their inquiry with great questions. He allowed His learners to explore solutions. He encouraged application[7] and much more.

He used many techniques that you as a communicator can intersect to maximize your message, whomever your audience. Of course, Jesus had none of the limitations we have. He was God and perfectly understood human nature. He never preached a boring sermon or taught a lifeless lesson. Yet, we can still learn from His example for God has given believers the mind of Christ (1 Cor. 2:16) and the Holy Spirit as our teacher (John 14:26).

That's what this book is all about … how you can successfully engage your audience with eight core communication principles that are modeled, practiced, and embodied by Jesus and supported by the latest findings from cognitive neuroscience and cognitive psychology about how we learn. Cognitive neuroscience helps us know where and how cognitive processes

---

[5] *Teaching as Jesus Taught by Roy B. Zuck (9-Jan-2002) Paperback* (Wipf & Stock Publishers, 2002), p. 24.

[6] *Zuck,* p. 17.

[7] HeeKap Lee, "Jesus Teaching Through Discovery," *International Christian Community of Teacher Educators Journal* 1, no. 2 (2016): 9.

occur in the brain, whereas cognitive psychology helps us understand mental processes and the behavior that follows, though both disciplines overlap.

In God's hands, we communicators become what neuroscientist Norman Doidge calls neuroplasticians.[8] Preaching, teaching, speechmaking, and training effect neuroplasticity, the ability God gave the brain to physically change itself in response to internal and external stimuli. Neuroplasticity is *the* fundamental process behind learning because learning actually changes the neural circuitry of our brains.

Research informs us that when communicators learn how the brain works and how to apply brain insight to communication, learning, and teaching, we become better communicators.[9] So, the neuroscience of learning provides one of the key foundations for this book.

These core principles answer the following eight crucial questions every communicator must ask and answer about their audience and themselves to give an effective speech, sermon, lesson, talk, or training session.

1. *Where do you want to take your audience?*
2. *How can you get your audience to really listen to you?*
3. *Why should your audience listen (the "so what" question)?*
4. *How can you beat the competition vying for the attention of your audience?*
5. *How can you help your audience feel your message?*

---

[8] Doidge, Norman, *The Brain That Changes Itself: Stories of Personal Triumph from the Frontiers of Brain Science,* (NY: Penguin Books, 2007), Kindle e-book loc. 204.

[9] Ranjini Mahinda JohnBull, Mariale M Hardiman, and Luke Rinne, "Professional Development Effects on Teacher Efficacy: Exploring How Knowledge of Neuro- and Cognitive Sciences Changes Beliefs and Practice," April 2013, 29.

6. *How can you help your message stick in the minds and hearts of your audience better?*
7. *How can you help those in your audience believe they can change and do what you suggest?*
8. *What does your audience need to do after your speech, sermon, lesson, or training session?*

Here are the eight core communication principles from the teachings of Jesus and how they are supported by neuroscience in answering those eight questions.

1. Clarity: Jesus began with the end in mind because He knew where He wanted to take His listeners. (Answers the *Where do you want to take your audience?* question.)
2. Attention: Jesus masterfully piqued people's interest to focus their attention on His message. (Answers the *How can you get your audience to listen to you?* question.)
3. Affinity: Jesus knew how to create a connection to His audience that prompted many to hear and heed what He said. (Answers the *Why should they listen to you?* question.)
4. Capacity: Jesus helped His listeners' minds stay engaged as He spoke. (Answers the *How can you beat the competition vying for the attention of your audience?* question.)
5. Durability: Jesus helped His listeners remember what He said so they could later recall it and act upon it. (Answers the *How can you help your message stick in the minds of your audience better?* question.)
6. Emotion: Jesus engaged people's hearts which cemented their learning. (Answers the *How can you help your audience feel your message?* question.)

7. Mindset: Jesus cultivated His listeners' confidence in Himself and in His message. (Answers the *How can you help those in your audience believe they can change or do what you suggest?* question.)
8. Transfer: Jesus stimulated personal application that led to life transformation. (Answers the *What does your audience need to do?* question.)

I combine these principles into this diagram I call the Healthy Learning Platter.

THE HEALTHY LEARNING PLATTER

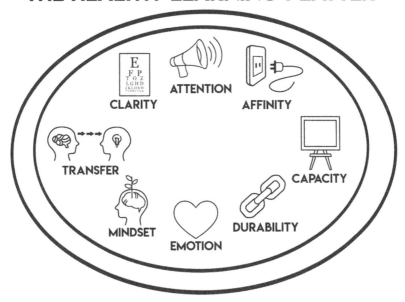

So, two sources of truth, the Bible and brain science, provide the backbone for this book. I intersect what we learn from Jesus' teaching recorded in the Gospels (how He spoke, what He spoke, and how others responded to His teaching) with insight on the latest neuroscience of learning. Both inform us about how to communicate well. I use neuroscience as a source of truth, taking a cue St. Augustine is first credited with saying, "All truth is God's truth."

However, a qualifier is in order. Some take Augustine's statement to equate human truth (i.e., science) with God's truth. That's not what he meant. God's Word is the ultimate authority on truth as it relates to eternal matters, yet it was never meant to provide us with every factual truth about all things. We can learn from both, as Dr. John Polkinghorne, former professor of mathematical physics at Cambridge University and the president of Queens' College, Cambridge, wrote, "Science and theology have things to say to each other, since both are concerned with the search for truth attained through motivated belief."[10]

Another important qualifier is this, "Our culture and historical distance from first-century Palestine makes a simple transfer of Jesus' approach [to communicating] to our own varied situations," challenging.[11] This simple truth reflects my intent in this book. Jesus modeled many communication techniques, the general sense of which we can apply to our modern-day settings.

* * *

An organization called TED provides some of the most admired and watched speeches today. TED brings speakers to the stage to present talks on various subjects in 18 minutes or less. These talks have been viewed online over a billion times. The head of TED, Chris Andersen, in his book, *TED Talks:*

---

[10] John Polkinghorne, "The Science and Religion Debate - an Introduction," January 1, 2007, https://www.researchgate.net/publication/251667290_The_Science_and_Religion_Debate_-_an_Introduction.

[11] Keith Ferdinando, "Jesus, the Theological Educator," *Themelios* 38, no. 3 (2013): 360–74.

The Official Guide to Public Speaking, calls the concept behind great presentation skills, *presentation literacy*. The old-fashioned name for these skills is rhetoric.[12] Even in antiquity, famous people valued presentation skills. Aristotle believed that effective persuasion included three components, ethos (credibility), logos (logic and data), and pathos (emotional appeal), which I write about in the pages that follow.

You might wonder what makes me qualified to write such a book. Well, I'm first and foremost a communicator. I make my living communicating as a pastor. With 40 years of ministry behind me and a few thousand sermons to boot, I've experienced much as a communicator, both effective and, let's just say, not so effective. In addition to my four degrees (one an executive masters in the neuroscience of leadership), I also earned a graduate certificate from Johns Hopkins University in *Mind, Brain, and Teaching,* and I'm currently completing my PhD.

I understand how learning happens in the brain, and I understand the challenge we communicators face. As a pastor who has averaged 15 hours a week preparing sermons, I've often wondered how much my teaching really sticks in my listeners' minds. Part of the problem for me and most other communicators lies in the wide range of our audiences. Who in our audience should we target? A Sunday worship service audience might include new believers, non-believers, mature believers, and everybody in between. How does a pastor connect to everybody? Perhaps the most fundamental question is, "Can I connect?" The answer is, "Yes," and I'll tackle that subject later in the book.

---

[12] Chris Anderson, *TED Talks: The Official TED Guide to Public Speaking*, Reprint edition (Mariner Books, 2017), Kindle e-book loc. 92.

Research indicates that most people quickly forget sermons. In one study of Catholic churchgoers, they could recall almost nothing about the priests' sermons.[13] In another study of Protestant churchgoers from a large church, researchers studied how PowerPoint slides might enhance retention and recall of the pastor's sermon.[14] They discovered that although churchgoers *felt* the PowerPoint slides helped, they actually didn't help them retain any more of the pastor's sermon. And in yet another study, researchers predicted that memory for religious messages would increase as a function of several variables: verbal ability, interest in the message, religiosity, and the consistency of the message with the religious beliefs of the subject. Again, the congregation in this study retained little from the sermons they heard.[15]

Schoolteachers often struggle to make their teaching stick. Businesspeople face an ongoing challenge to get their message out, train their employees, and cast vision for their companies. Speechmakers spend hours prepping their talks and often don't know what will eventually stick in the minds of their audience. Sunday school teachers may also wonder how well their lessons connect to their students.

Perhaps you've felt a similar frustration as I have, wondering just how well your lesson, sermon, talk, or training

---

[13] Chris A M Hermans and Anneke Mooij, "Memory of Deductive and Inductive Sermons: Empirical Research in the Effects of Transmission of Theological Concepts in the Doctrinal Mode," *Journal of Empirical Theology* 23, no. 2 (2010): 201–31, https://doi.org/10.1163/157092510X527358.

[14] Aaron Buchko, Kathleen Buchko, and Joseph Meyer, "Perceived Efficacy and the Actual Effectiveness of PowerPoint on the Retention and Recall of Religious Messages in the Weekly Sermon: An Empirical Field Study," *Journal of Communication & Religion* 36, no. 3 (December 2013): 149–65.

[15] Kenneth I Pargament and Donald V DeRosa, "What Was That Sermon about: Predicting Memory for Religious Messages from Cognitive Psychology Theory," *Journal for the Scientific Study of Religion* 24, no. 2 (June 1985): 180–93.

session connected. Our frustrations are not unfounded. Communicators face many challenges in our world today, including fragmented attention, multi-tasking mania, and increased forgetting, among others.

External stimuli increasingly bombard us 24/7. Linda Stone, a former executive with Microsoft, coined the phrase, "continuous partial attention."[16] She defines continuous partial attention this way, "to keep a top-level item in focus and constantly scan the periphery in case something more important emerges." As a result, our attention is constantly scattered, which negatively impacts learning.

Many believe the neuromyth that we can multi-task—do two things at once that require our attention (we can't).[17] Multi-taskers incessantly tab shift, task switch, and notification check, all of which diminishes attention and learning in the moment and carries over into learning environments where we attempt to get a message across to others. Such task-switching leaves little time for the deep processing needed for enduring learning.

We live in a world that increasingly forgets. Unfortunately, those who passively listen to us forget most of what we say. In the late 1800s and early 1900s, a German psychologist named Hermann Ebbinghaus researched memory. He created over 2,000 short nonsense words and experimented on himself by memorizing lists of them and then recorded how long it took him to forget them. Out of his research rose what psychologists call *the forgetting curve*. Although only one person participated in his research, himself, his findings have generally stood to

---

[16] Linda Stone, "Continuous Partial Attention," Linda Stone, accessed May 3, 2013, http://lindastone.net/qa/continuous-partial-attention/.

[17] Nancy Napier, "The Myth of Multitasking," *Psychology Today*, May 12, 2014, http://www.psychologytoday.com/blog/creativity-without-borders/201405/the-myth-multitasking.

this day.[18] Simply put, if we passively engage in learning, we quickly forget what we learn. Most people will forget 70% of a talk within 24 hours and up to 90% within a week.

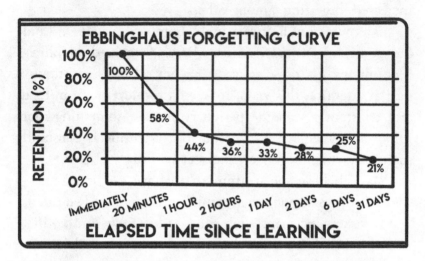

James even reminds us about the peril of forgetting when he writes, "But don't just listen to God's word. You must do what it says. Otherwise, you are only fooling yourselves. For if you listen to the word and don't obey, it is like glancing at your face in a mirror. You see yourself, walk away, and forget what you look like" (James 1:22-24, NLT).

These frustrations motivated me to write this book to provide communicators with practical tools gleaned from the latest neuroscience of learning and illustrated in the life of the Master Teacher Himself—Jesus. So, whether you are a teacher who teaches, a leader who leads, a preacher who preaches, a speaker who speaks, or simply a learner who learns, if you apply these eight principles, you will communicate and learn better.

---

[18] Jaap M. J. Murre and Joeri Dros, "Replication and Analysis of Ebbinghaus' Forgetting Curve," *PLoS ONE* 10, no. 7 (July 6, 2015), https://doi.org/10.1371/journal.pone.0120644.

Ultimately, however, Christian communicators must remember that God's Kingdom is not about a perfectly crafted sermon, lesson, talk, or training lesson based on the neuroscience and psychology of learning. It involves much more. God ultimately effects lasting learning and transformation. As the Apostle Paul wrote, "For the kingdom of God is not a matter of talk but of power" (1 Cor. 4:20).

Not every communication insight will directly apply to your setting, nor does every technique produce equal results. Certain techniques will work better in some settings than others. And some techniques will work more effectively in one learner and perhaps not so much in another.

To avoid cumbersome repetition, each time I refer to a communicator's speech, sermon, lesson, talk, or training session, I will simply use the word "talk" to refer to them all. I will use the term "communicator" as a catch-all term for teachers, preachers, speech makers, and business leaders. Also, for simplicity's sake, I will use the word "learner" to refer to a church congregant, student, employee at a training session, pupil, etc.

I weave four components throughout this book: story, Scripture, science, and skill. I share several stories, some personal and some not. I imbed Scriptures, especially those that illustrate how Jesus taught. I support my ideas with the latest neuroscience findings about how we learn. And finally, I suggest some skills and tools you can use to maximize your communication effectiveness.

Each chapter begins with a preview and ends with a summary (a good communication practice). I've also provided several downloadable tools at this www.charlesstone.com/TEDfreebies to help you become a better communicator.

Because I hope to maximize your learning as you read, I've applied some neuroscience learning principles that decades of research have underscored.[19] One concept, pre-encoding, simply means "tell 'em what you are going to tell 'em before you tell 'em." So, I've summarized the eight principles here along with three practices for each principle that I'll unpack in future chapters. Reading this now will help prime your brain to learn better. Neurons (brain cells) that are excited before a learning experience are more likely to be allocated to memory traces in subsequent learning experiences. So, "telling 'em before you tell 'em" has a sound brain basis.[20] Also, at the website www.charlesstone.com/TEDfreebies. I've provided a downloadable outline of all these principles you may want to refer to as you read the book.

So, here are the eight principles with three related practices for each one.

PRINCIPLE 1: CLARITY—BEGIN WITH THE END IN MIND

1. Clarify the big take-away(s).
2. Create a concept map.
3. Capitalize on the primacy-recency principle.

---

[19] Camille A. Farrington et al., *Teaching Adolescents To Become Learners The Role of Noncognitive Factors in Shaping School Performance: A Critical Literature Review* (Chicago: Consortium On Chicago School Research, 2013), p. 36.

[20] Talya Sadeh et al., "Overlap between Hippocampal Pre-Encoding and Encoding Patterns Supports Episodic Memory," *Hippocampus* 29, no. 9 (2019): 836–47, https://doi.org/10.1002/hipo.23079.

PRINCIPLE 2: ATTENTION—PIQUE INTEREST

1. Adapt your material to the dynamics of attention.
2. Add the appropriate attention-grabber(s).
3. Apply the concept of priming.

PRINCIPLE 3: AFFINITY—CREATE CONNECTION

1. Know your material.
2. Know your audience.
3. Help the audience know (and like) you.

PRINCIPLE 4: CAPACITY—FREE UP WORKING MEMORY

1. Maximize all the components of working memory.
2. Minimize cognitive load.
3. Marry new knowledge to prior knowledge.

PRINCIPLE 5: DURABILITY—STIMULATE LONG-TERM MEMORY

1. Concentrate on enhancing recall.
2. Choose sticky memory techniques.
3. Create "aha" moments.

PRINCIPLE 6: EMOTION—ENGAGE THE HEART

1. Leverage emotional learning.
2. Limit cognitive dissonance.
3. Lead with well-placed stories.

PRINCIPLE 7: MINDSET—CULTIVATE CONFIDENCE

1. Avoid the big neuromyths.
2. Act with a contagious spirit.
3. Accelerate learner motivation.

PRINCIPLE 8: TRANSFER—STIMULATE LIFE APPLICATION

1. Clarify the "Now What?"
2. Create clear cues.
3. Count on the work of the Holy Spirit.

* * *

Before I delve into these principles, I will deal with two important subjects in the next two chapters. The first chapter will define concepts behind learning. The chapter that follows will unpack the different kinds of memory and explain why understanding memory is crucial to making your talks stick in your learners' minds and hearts.

Check out the website for downloadable tools at
www.charlesstone.com/TEDfreebies

2

Learning: Then and Now

The one who does the work does the learning. [21]

—Terry Doyle

It was 1933, and he was only seven when a bike ran over him. After it hit him, his head smashed against the ground, and he lay unconscious a few minutes. Little did he know that in the years ahead, he would inadvertently teach the world more about learning, memory, and the brain than perhaps any other person on the planet.

Seizures began soon after his accident, and initially, they were manageable with medication. But they grew worse over time, and at age 27, he had 10 seizures a day, even with the large dosages of anti-convulsant medication given to him. A renowned neurosurgeon at the time, Dr. William Scoville, suggested experimental surgery in hopes of diminishing his seizures.

The surgery, performed in 1953, removed parts of both temporal lobes of his brain (the temporal lobes are highly involved in memory). It did reduce the number of his seizures to only five small ones each month, but the doctor quickly discovered a tragic side effect. The man could no longer create

---

[21] Terry Doyle and John Tagg, *Helping Students Learn in a Learner-Centered Environment: A Guide to Facilitating Learning in Higher Education* (Sterling, Va: Stylus Publishing, 2008), p. 63.

any new memories (called anterograde amnesia). He did, however, retain most of his childhood memories, including the bicycle accident, who his family was, and who he was.

He was known as Patient H.M. until after his death when his full name, Henry Molaison, was revealed. He lived in a care institute in Connecticut from 1957 until his death in 2008. While there, he was widely studied. And although his working memory (where we store and manipulate information for a few seconds) and procedural memory (where memories of habits like how to ride a bike reside) were intact, he could not remember any new facts.

For example, his primary researcher, Canadian neuropsychologist Brenda Milner, would come into this room, introduce herself to him, leave the room, and return a few minutes later. Each time, Henry would treat her as if he had never met her. Even after 30 years, he still could not recall her name. He lived what neuroscientist and learning expert Stanislas Dehaene describes as, "an eternal present, unable to add the slightest new memory to his mental biography."[22]

After scientists studied Henry for decades and after studying his brain after his death, scientists discovered much about how the brain learns and remembers. For example, we've learned that the brain stores and manipulates different kinds of memory in different places (i.e., learning new facts depends on structures called the hippocampus, working memory, and pre-frontal cortex). And depending on what we are learning (conscious or unconscious), the brain uses different kinds of learning systems.

---

[22] Stanislas Dehaene, *How We Learn: Why Brains Learn Better Than Any Machine . . . for Now* (New York, New York: Viking, 2020), p. 91.

What Is Learning? [23]

To most effectively get our message across when we communicate, we must understand both learning and memory because they are both tightly linked. As educational expert David Sousa writes, "Learning is the process by which we acquire new knowledge and skills; memory is the process by which we retain [them]."[24] Although I touch on memory in this chapter, I devote the entire next chapter to it.

**BASIC CLASSIFICATION OF
MEMORY STORAGE**

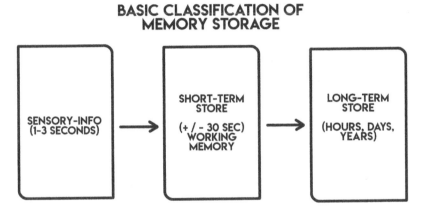

Learning is measured in two ways—what you retain (remembering stuff) and transfer (using that stuff to solve new problems in different contexts). It involves three kinds of memory storage, including sensory memory (which briefly holds visual or auditory sensory images and can last up to

---

[23] In a book on communication, I must at least mention several learning theorists familiar to educators who have influenced thinking about learning: Vygotsky (social constructivism), Skinner (behaviorism), Piaget (cognitive constructivism), Knowles (andragogy), Mezirow (transformative learning), Wenger (social learning), Schon (reflective-change learning), and Bloom (Bloom's taxonomy, a way of looking at learning through a hierarchy from lower-order thinking skills to higher-order thinking skills).

[24] David A. Sousa, *How the Brain Learns*, 5th edition (Thousand Oaks, CA: Corwin, 2016), p. 86.

three or four seconds, think of the light trail a moving sparkler leaves), working memory, of which short-term memory is a component (it allows us to store and manipulate a few pieces of information for up to 30 seconds or so such as when you remember a telephone number long enough to dial it), and long-term memory (which is virtually unlimited and stores knowledge in a more or less permanent way, such as when you recall your first-grade teacher's name).

Fundamentally, learning means to acquire new information (knowledge, skills, or attitudes), and memory allows us to receive, record, and recall this information later. We might say that memory is the byproduct of learning—the record of learning stored in our brains. If we have truly learned something, our brain physically changes (called neuroplasticity), which allows us to later retrieve what we've learned if it's been stored strongly enough (called encoding).

Learning doesn't happen magically or passively. The Holy Spirit does not force learning on us by making our neural circuits change without our cooperation, neither does learning happen without intentional effort (called explicit or conscious learning). The exception to intentional learning occurs when something traumatic happens to us or when we experience a deeply emotional event which causes what is called intrinsic or unconscious learning. Such learning happens without our intention to learn.

At the brain level, a simple view of learning is that neurons and groups of neurons get connected to each other better, which is called synaptic strengthening. The main brain cell involved in learning is called the neuron, and the stronger the connections between neurons due to more dendrites being formed (tiny projections from the cell, think branches of a tree), the deeper the learning. A synapse is the connection between neurons, although neurons don't actually touch each other. The term for this strengthening process is called long-term potentiation, and the term for weakening these connections (linked to forgetting) is called long-term depression. Some neurons can have as many as 40 dendritic branches[25] and can connect to as many at 10,000 other neurons.

One way to view communication between neurons is to imagine lips whispering something close to another person's ear. The upstream neuron sends a signal (the lips). Between each neuronal projection is a space called a synaptic cleft (the space between the lips and ear). The downstream neuron receives the signal (the ear).[26]

At this cellular level, learning and memory essentially change the *chemicals* within and between neurons as well as physically alter the synaptic *connections* between neurons. One connection may get stronger and more easily excite the next neuron (long-term potentiation), whereas another connection may get weaker (long-term depression) and excite the next neuron a bit less. An appropriate cue in the future will trigger those neurons to fire so we can retrieve that memory of what we learned.

When we repeatedly activate these neural circuits through learning, they strengthen, and these patterns of connectivity that underlie memory traces are called *engrams*. But we must forget some stuff along the way, or our brains would keep growing within the limited space inside our skull. Our heads would literally explode if they kept on growing.

Dr. Donald Hebb (1904–1985), a Canadian psychologist who studied how neurons affect learning, is known for what is called Hebb's Law. He theorized that when neurons consistently "fire together, they wire together." In other words, when

[25] Kandel, *In Search of Memory,* p. 65.
[26] Kandel, p. 65.

we pay attention and keep paying attention, learning happens because new pathways and synapses (connections between neurons, even though they don't actually touch) are more or less permanently formed.[27] "A synapse that gets stronger is like a factory that increases its productivity; it recruits more neurotransmitters on the presynaptic side and more receptor molecules on the postsynaptic side."[28]

This process is the essence of neuroplasticity,[29] the brain's ability to change in response to stimuli. As one neuroscientist said, our brains are more flexible than we ever thought, more like Play-Doh than porcelain.[30]

Recently, however, neuroscientists discovered an additional neuroplastic process involved in learning, called intrinsic plasticity.[31] So apparently, two processes at the neuronal level affect learning, synaptic neuroplasticity (changes between neurons) and intrinsic plasticity (changes within the neuron itself).

Given this brief explanation of changes that happen at the neuronal level when we learn, how might we define learning? I'll suggest several angles. Neuroscientist Thad Polk defines

---

[27] This is long-term potentiation (LTP). When a neuron repeatedly fires, in the future when it fires, it takes less frequent firing for the receiving neuron to itself fire. The receiving neuron takes less signaling from the sending neuron to be activated.

[28] Dehaene, *How We Learn*, p. 94.

[29] Notable people associated with neuroplasticity throughout history include the Apostle Paul (1st century, the first neuroplastician), William James (1842-1910), Ramoni y Cajal (discovered neurons, 1852-1934), Donald Hebb (1904-1985), Ed Taub (from his late 70s research on Makake monkeys, 1931-) and Michael Merzenick (1942-) and J. H. Kass.

[30] John J. Ratey, *Spark: The Revolutionary New Science of Exercise and the Brain*, Reprint (NY, NY: Little, Brown and Company, 2013), p. 35.

[31] Hyun Geun Shim, Yong-Seok Lee, and Sang Jeong Kim, "The Emerging Concept of Intrinsic Plasticity: Activity-Dependent Modulation of Intrinsic Excitability in Cerebellar Purkinje Cells and Motor Learning," *Experimental Neurobiology* 27, no. 3 (June 2018): 139–54, https://doi.org/10.5607/en.2018.27.3.139.

learning as, "acquiring knowledge or behavioral responses from experience."[32] Experience might come from studying, reading, life experience, or being taught in a class or a seminar. By this definition, instincts and reflexes don't actually count as learning. Mental activity must actually happen in a learner's brain for durable learning to occur.[33]

Another angle that helps define learning relates to long-term memory—what stays in our noggin for months, years, or a lifetime. Nothing truly gets learned unless long-term memory gets changed. Educational specialist David Didau defines learning as, "the ability to retain skills and knowledge over the *long term* and to be able to transfer them to new contexts."[34]

One final way to define learning is to describe it with this formula: learning = memory + attention + engagement.[35] In the chapters that follow, I'll unpack each of these components.

Not only is it helpful to define learning, but it's also helpful to understand the basic steps we (especially adult learners) navigate to learn. Professors David Taylor and Hossam Hamdy suggest that adults learn through these steps.[36] The steps occur whether your talk is a one-off (a one-hour training session) or a series of classes.

---

[32] Dr. Thad A Polk, *The Learning Brain*, The Great Courses (Chantilly, VA: The Great Courses, 2018), p. 6.

[33] Richard E. Mayer, ed., *The Cambridge Handbook of Multimedia Learning*, 2 edition (New York: Cambridge University Press, 2014), p. 22.

[34] David Didau, *What If Everything You Knew About Education Was Wrong?* (UK: Learning Sciences International, 2019), p. 169.

[35] Glenn Whitman and Ian Kelleher, *Neuroteach: Brain Science and the Future of Education* (Lanham, Maryland: Rowman & Littlefield Publishers, 2016), Kindle e-book loc. 1980.

[36] David C. M. Taylor and Hossam Hamdy, "Adult Learning Theories: Implications for Learning and Teaching in Medical Education: AMEE Guide No. 83," *Medical Teacher* 35, no. 11 (November 2013): e1561–72, https://doi.org/10.3109/0142159X.2013.828153.

1. All learning starts with prior learning.
2. Dissonance occurs next when existing knowledge is challenged and seen to be incomplete.
3. Next comes refinement when the learner practices elaboration, looking at possible solutions or explanations. Out of this arise new concepts for the learner.
4. In the next phase, organization, the learner accommodates the new information by developing or restructuring their ideas by looking at it from different perspectives.
5. Feedback follows. The learner will test their new knowledge against what others may believe (the teacher, fellow students, people in their church small group, etc.).
6. The final phase, consolidation, happens when the learner looks back over their learning to identify what they've learned to see how it fits within the big picture.

With this in mind, communicators can help learners along this pathway articulate what they know (prior knowledge), keep in mind their learning preferences and motivations, and help them consider other resources to aid learning. In the pages that follow, I'll articulate these in more detail.

* * *

Not only does neuroscience tell us much about learning, the New Testament does as well. As I noted earlier, the New Testament records that the disciples addressed Jesus as "Teacher," and He accepted this designation (John 13:13). He also added the self-designation, "Lord." In the Greek New Testament text, the Gospels calls Jesus Teacher 45 times, and they give the term "disciple" or "learner" to His followers 214 times.[37] In general, the Gospel writers describe Jesus' ministry as three-fold—teaching, preaching, and healing, all of which embody communication in some way (Matt. 4:23; 9:35). The first two do so with words, and the latter—healing—via actions which were often preceded by words.

In Matthew 13:13-15, Jesus differentiated between merely hearing and true understanding. Hearing involved only their heads but true understanding (learning) involved their hearts as well. The Greek word for learning, *manthano,* occurs 25 times in the New Testament and six times in the Gospels. Although it can range in meaning from knowing facts to true understanding, when Jesus said, "Take my yoke and *learn* from me," (Matt. 11:29), He probably used it in the latter way. "The disciples learning was not simply a cognitive process, but a reorientation of life, values, and character, through experiencing the *life* of Christ quite as much as through hearing His words."[38]

How Learning Has Changed Since Jesus' Day

It's best to view Jesus' teaching techniques from a broad rather than a detailed perspective to avoid the risk of making applications that we can't honestly make. Today's world differs dramatically from the biblical world. Even so, our brains are essentially the same which means humans learned then and now in similar ways. Only the context has changed. Teachers in Jesus' day, primarily the rabbis, practiced some of the same characteristics that today's communicators can also practice.

---

[37] Naugle, p. 9.
[38] Keith Ferdinando, "Jesus, the Theological Educator," *Themelios* 38, no. 3 (2013): 360–74.

Learned rabbis not only knew their material well but were skilled in the art of presentation.[39]

So how did Jesus' environment, tools, and methods differ from today?

First, Jesus held no classes in formal classrooms as we would define them today. He taught in multiple places—the synagogue (Mark 6:2), on a mountain (Matt. 5:1), and in desert places (Mark 6:34-35). In fact, one popular teaching technique was called *peripatetic teaching*, teaching by walking around. That is, a rabbi would set up a small school and have his students tag along as he walked around and did life. Today, most of our teaching and communication happens in fixed places like schoolrooms, churches, auditoriums, and board rooms. And in the 21st century, seldom do communicators live with their students to create a 24/7 learning experience as Jesus did with His disciples.

Yet during New Testament times, formal schooling began to appear when Jewish boys would go to a central location to be taught, much like an elementary school today. These schools were probably found in most Palestinian towns.[40] Writing could be done on a wooden tablet. The textbooks were the Law, the Prophets, and writings that became the Old Testament. The brightest boys, like the Apostle Paul, would later go to Jerusalem to one of the few formal schools.[41]

---

[39] Mr. Birger Gerhardsson and Mr. Jacob Neusner, *Memory and Manuscript with Tradition and Transmission in Early Christianity*, trans. Mr. Eric J. Sharpe, Revised edition (Grand Rapids, MI: Wm. B. Eerdmans-Lightning Source, 1998), p. 110.

[40] Gerhardsson and Neusner, p. 22.

[41] Patricia Bennett, "Seasoned with Salt: An Exploration of the Teaching Techniques of the Master Teacher, Jesus Christ, to Determine Their Correlation with a Variety of Individual Learning Styles" (2012), https://www.semanticscholar. org/paper/Seasoned-with-Salt%3A-An-Exploration-of-the-Teaching-Bennett/4 9048a6862922093c6317b3d870144e773c8cb3e.

As far as we know, Jesus didn't create lesson plans, a curriculum, use notes, teach others how to teach, or require His disciples to take notes. His teaching was all oral, as educational institutes in antiquity favored oral learning, even in Greek culture. Yet even before Greek culture, education was important for the Jewish people. Jesus often went to the local synagogue, read a verse of Scripture, and then explain it. The Scriptures tell us that Jesus grew in wisdom (Luke 2:52), and He had probably memorized much of the Torah. His Heavenly Father did not perform a massive information download into Jesus' brain. Although fully God, Jesus chose to limit Himself to learn much like we do. And although Jesus didn't prepare His sermons and teaching ahead of time, we usually do today.

Jesus taught more informally, spontaneously, and impromptu. Although He began His teaching ministry in the Synagogue, because the Jewish spiritual leaders resisted Him, He spent most of His time teaching outdoors. As He taught informally, He often did so in informal places. As far as we know, Jesus gave out no *written* assignments. His exams were mostly oral and informal. His exams were often assignments to go and do what He said. Today, however, most communicators don't regularly speak off the cuff, and most teachers give exams.

Jesus used no technology that we commonly use today when we bring a talk. Although during the New Testament era, literacy was not as high as it is today (most people today can read and write), it was higher in the Greek and Jewish culture. Jews may have been the most literate group in the Roman empire, and reading and writing could have been considered cutting-edge technology in their day.

Some, perhaps, may have used a form of a notebook that they would carry, "for their day-to-day business, perhaps hung at the belt, jotting down a few of the striking sayings they had heard or writing a summary of what they had experienced while it was fresh in the memory."[42]

The Jewish historian Josephus noted that the Jews took pride in educating their children, and the law was their textbook.[43] Although less could write, many could read, and many memorized the Torah. Men were generally more literate than women because only boys received formal training. Men would read from the Scriptures in the synagogue, and a quorum of 10 men who could read the Torah was required to start a synagogue. Memorizing Scripture was very important.

The Jews used a fundamental learning technique which enabled them to memorize—repetition. A teacher would read the text out loud over and over until the students learned it by heart. Pious Jews would memorize the Torah which would have required extensive repetition.[44]

However, Jesus' teaching differed from the rabbis in a significant way. The rabbis focused on remembering the law. Jesus focused on His disciples becoming more like Him. The rabbis emphasized memorization. Jesus emphasized reasoning and heart-to-heart communication. The rabbis sought behavior change. Jesus sought to integrate behavior with heart, both the visible and the invisible. Finally, the rabbis wanted their learners to master content. Jesus sought transformed lives as His learners applied content.[45]

* * *

---

[42] Alan Millard, *Reading and Writing in the Time of Jesus* (New York: NYU Press, 2000), p. 223.

[43] Craig A. Evans, *The World of Jesus and the Early Church* (Hendrickson Publishers, 2011), p. 83.

[44] Gerhardsson and Neusner, p. 29.

[45] HeeKap Lee, "Jesus Teaching Through Discovery," *International Christian Community of Teacher Educators Journal* 1, no. 2 (2006): 9.

Between 1997 and 2004, the late Professor Graham Nuthall of Canterbury University in New Zealand conducted some of the most robust research ever on learning.[46] His Project on Learning, a long-term study of students ages 9 to 11, examined what students actually retained in the classroom experience. He wired 12 different classrooms with video cameras and microphones to record what happened. As a result of his research, he could predict with 80-85 percent accuracy what students learned. Some of his findings included:

- A third of what students learn will be unique to them and not known by the other students.
- Students will tend to know 40-50 percent of what we're trying to teach them, but they all don't know the same 40-50 percent.
- If a student encounters a concept on at least three different occasions, their chance of remembering it six months later rockets to 80 percent.
- Much of what students learn they learn from each other, and 80 percent is wrong.
- Learning doesn't happen because something was taught but as a result of how students *experience* learning.

What Are the Implications of This Research for Us?

For communicators to foster learning, we must remember that learning is a far more mysterious experience than simply using a few communication techniques. In this book, I don't suggest learning will automatically happen in the learners in your context if you apply these techniques. However, neuroscience informs us, and Jesus illustrates to us how we can best

---

[46] Didau, pp. 183-188.

effect durable learning. But ultimately, it requires a learner's active engagement and the work of the Holy Spirit to effect transformation.

So, as you read this book, allow these broad ideas to frame your learning.[47] I will expand on each in future chapters:

1. Learning engages the total person (thinking, feeling, and physically doing).
2. The brain seeks patterns to find meaning.
3. Emotions powerfully affect learning.
4. Past learning impacts future learning.
5. Memory (working memory) has a limited functional capacity.
6. You must rehearse to retain.
7. Practice makes permanent, not perfect.

* * *

---

[47] Sousa, p. 214.

APPLICATION

1. Without re-reading the chapter, take two minutes and write down everything you can recall. You can use this technique, called free recall, with your learners in your talks.
2. Based on your reading, how would you define learning for your context?
3. Can you complete this fundamental rule of learning I wrote about from Dr. Donald Hebb? And define what this rule means—*Neurons that fire together, _____ together.*

Check out the website for downloadable tools at
www.charlesstone.com/TEDfreebies

3

Memory and Why It Matters

We are who we are because of what we learn and what we remember. —Eric Kandel, Nobel Prize Winner[48]

Memory is the cabinet of the imagination, the treasury of reason, the registry of conscience, and the council chamber of thought. —St. Basil

Memory is the residue of thought.
—Dr. Daniel T. Willingham[49]

Think about the most memorable class, sermon, or speech you can recall. What made it so memorable? The answer lies in the word "memorable" which comes from the word

---

[48] Kandel, p. 10.
[49] Daniel T. Willingham, *Why Don't Students Like School?: A Cognitive Scientist Answers Questions About How the Mind Works and What It Means for the Classroom*, 1 edition (Wiley, 2009), p. 53.

"memory."[50] You would not be able to recall that class, sermon, or speech without memory. Without memory, nothing gets learned.

Without memory, we could not solve problems we face in everyday life. Without memory, we could not create a coherent picture of the past that gives us perspective for current life. Without memory, the experiences of life would simply be a hodgepodge of splintered fragments. Without memory, life would have no perceived continuity. Without memory, we could not read or understand the Bible. Without memory, you would not be reading this book. As noble prize winner Eric Kandel writes, "All human accomplishments, from antiquity to modern times, are products of a shared memory accumulated over centuries, whether through written records or through a carefully protected oral tradition."[51]

The first thing we do when we don't know something or when we try to solve a problem is search our memory banks for information. Educational expert Daniel Willingham notes, "Memory is the cognitive [mental] process of first resort."[52] So,

---

[50] Several leading scientists have uniquely contributed to our understanding of memory. Their work has influenced how I've approached memory in this book. Dr. Donald Hebb is known for his research on neurons and learning and the phrase, "Neurons the fire together wire together." Dr. Alan Pavio is known for "dual-coding," the theory that verbal and non-verbal information is stored separately in long-term memory. Dr. Nelson Cowan's research resulted in the view that working memory has a capacity of four items, plus or minus one. Drs. Richard Shiffrin and Richard Atkinson asserted that three components form memory: a sensory register, a short-term store, and a long-term store. Dr. Alan Baddeley is known for the four-part model of working memory (the central executive, the phonological loop, the episodic buffer, and the visuospatial sketchpad). Dr. John Sweller is known for "cognitive load theory," which posits that in several ways we can overload the capacity for learners to learn. And of course, Nobel laureate (2000) Dr. Eric R. Kandel must make this list for his research on sea slugs (aplysia) that lead to his seminal findings on memory.

[51] Kandel, p. 10.

[52] Willingham, *Why Don't Students Like School?*, p 37.

when communicators gain a basic understanding of memory, they communicate more effectively.

Multimedia Learning and Memory

God did not design us to learn in a single-channel, unlimited-capacity, passive way. That is, He did not create our brains to process all information in the same way. We process the visual different from the verbal, and we can't process an unlimited amount of information in our memory. Our brains don't work like human tape recorders, passively taking in and recording everything our minds get exposed to.[53]

Again, learning does not happen without memory, and most learning today comes in some way via a multimedia medium—in a talk that uses PowerPoint slides, an online lesson with animations, a lesson or sermon with show-and-tell items, etc. As a result, psychologists have developed what is called the *theory of multimedia learning* which explains what happens in your learners' brains and memories when you communicate via multimedia. Three assumptions underlie this view of learning.[54]

First, learners process visual and verbal information in two different ways (i.e., through two different channels). Although the information may come through one channel (they see a picture of a dog, the visual channel), they process it in the other channel as well (they silently repeat the word "dog" to themselves, the verbal channel).

Second, they can process only a limited amount of information in each channel. When they hear a talk or see an animation, their brain doesn't record every word or image.

---

[53] Mayer, p. 46.
[54] Mayer, p. 47.

Rather, they pick and choose the words or images that make the most sense and that seem most important to them. The part of working memory (more on that below) called the *central executive* drives this picking and choosing process. Imagine the central executive like a symphony conductor who coordinates all the instruments in an orchestra or like a boss in a company that allocates company resources, co-ordinates activities, and prioritizes tasks. Fundamentally, this part of the brain directs our spotlight of attention—where we place our attention.

Third, durable learning requires that your learner actively engage in three ways. They must pay attention to incoming information (they select it). They must process it in ways that make sense to them (they organize it). Finally, they must combine that new information with prior knowledge which moves it into long-term memory (they integrate it).

Multimedia Learning

1. Learners process visual and verbal information through different neural channels.
2. Learners can process only a limited amount in each channel.
3. Learners engage information in three ways—they select it, they organize it, and they integrate it into their memory.

A learner will first pay attention to relevant words and images in your talk (selection). They will then make connections among selected words or images to create mental maps or models that make sense of the material (organizing). Finally, a learner will combine the visual and auditory material into a coherent whole. They will reach back into long-term memory to retrieve prior knowledge, bring that information into working memory, combine it with the new information, and then send the updated information back to long-term memory for long-term storage (integration).

This process, called *encoding*, happens when knowledge gets sent to long-term memory into models of understanding, called schemas. Imagine a schema like a manila folder with "dog" written on the tab. Within that folder, you've placed various pictures and articles about dogs. A schema would be like a neural manila folder in your brain with information about dogs. The processes involved in encoding, selecting, organizing, and integrating occur several times in your learner's mind during a talk.

So fundamentally, memories get stored when a learner can comprehend new information (it makes sense to them) and when they can connect it to past experiences (it has meaning to them).[55] Our overall goals for all of our talks should be that they make sense and give meaning to our learners. Also, keep in mind that research indicates memory guides our behavior in three ways—reflexes (don't touch a hot iron), habits that we do without thinking much, and goals (we anticipate a future outcome). And we tend to underestimate the impact of existing habits and reflexes and overestimate the importance of goals.[56]

[55] Oded Bein, Niv Reggev, and Anat Maril, "Prior Knowledge Influences on Hippocampus and Medial Prefrontal Cortex Interactions in Subsequent Memory," *Neuropsychologia* 64 (November 1, 2014): 320–30, https://doi.org/10.1016/j.neuropsychologia.2014.09.046.
[56] Carmen Simon, *Impossible to Ignore: Creating Memorable Content to Influence Decisions*, 1 edition (New York: McGraw-Hill Education, 2016), Kindle e-book locs. 197-235.

A Brief Primer on Memory

In the prior chapter, I briefly explained that scientists classify memory storage into three stages: stage one—sensory memory, stage two—working (short-term) memory, and stage three—long-term memory. Memory processing begins with sensory memory. Some of it makes it to short-term-memory, and even less makes it to long-term memory. What gets moved to the long-term memory depends on what learners pay attention to, its emotional content, and how important, interesting, relevant, or useful that information is to them (called salience). And although working memory's storage is limited and long-term memory is functionally unlimited, information can't bypass working memory on its way to long-term memory. Working memory can become a bottleneck, like road construction can slow traffic when a four-lane highway narrows to one lane. Later, I devote a whole chapter on how to minimize this bottleneck effect.

Working memory and short-term memory sometimes get confused with each other. Short-term memory is part of working memory. It stores information, whereas working memory both stores and manipulates it. Think of working memory as a mental sketch pad where you briefly hold information from both your environment and from existing memories while at the same time manipulating that information.

The diagram below pictures the three classifications of memory storage. I explain it in more detail in the pages that follow.

EXPANDED CLASSIFICATION OF MEMORY STORAGE

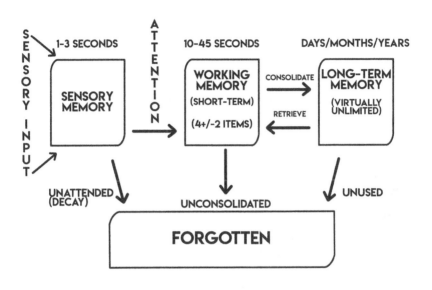

Sensory Memory

Sensory memory holds information for a fraction of a second up to a few seconds. A good example is the brief light trail a sparkler leaves when you move it around at night. Sensory memory processes information through our five senses—the way something looks, feels, sounds, etc. Sensory memory for visual stimuli is called iconic memory (the sparkler trail you soon forget), for auditory, echoic memory (the sound of the doorbell you soon forget), and for touch, haptic memory (the itch you just had that you forgot). Visual sensory memory lasts about one second while auditory memory can last up to four or five seconds.[57] This stage one memory gives the brain time to process incoming information, yet it's not consciously

---

[57] Mayer, p. 240.

controlled. And 99% of sensory memory is forgotten because it was not salient or important.[58]

Working (Short-Term) Memory

Working memory, sometimes called short-term memory, is not a passive storage system. It acts as short-term storage by pulling up other memories and manipulating them with new information and memories. It's like a mail shelf where an employee might pick up mail to make room for new deliveries. However, with this one, unless it's picked up, it gets thrown out because it won't stay in memory (on the shelf) very long.[59] It's limited in size, whereas long-term memory is virtually unlimited. It is involved in virtually everything we do, from remembering a phone number, to carrying on a conversation with another, to reading, driving, or praying. Working memory is a good indicator of raw intelligence. It involves what are called executive functions which include keeping information in working memory, inhibiting unnecessary information, and shifting our focus of attention.[60]

Several parts of the brain are involved in working memory, including the very front part of your brain called the pre-frontal cortex (PFC) and the part of the brain highly involved in short- and long-term memory, called the hippocampus. It takes lots of mental energy to keep information in

---

[58] Mariale M. Hardiman, *The Brain-Targeted Teaching Model for 21st-Century Schools*, 1 edition (Thousand Oaks, Calif: Corwin, 2012), Kindle e-book loc. 2089.

[59] Hilde Østby, Ylva Østby, and Sam Kean, *Adventures in Memory: The Science and Secrets of Remembering and Forgetting* (Greystone Books, 2018), p. 173.

[60] Emma Gregory et al., "Building Creative Thinking in the Classroom: From Research to Practice," *International Journal of Educational Research* 62 (January 1, 2013): 43–50, https://doi.org/10.1016/j.ijer.2013.06.003.

working memory, and sometimes, we can overload it with our talks. It's called cognitive load which I deal with later.

For information to make it to working memory, you must pay attention to the information coming from sensory memory. You can hold information in working memory for 10-45 seconds,[61] yet you can retrieve information very quickly, in less than 50 milliseconds (a millisecond is one thousandth of a second).[62] It serves as the intermediary between sensory and long-term memory and is involved in creating lasting memories.

How does working memory relate to short-term memory?[63] Short-term memory is a component process of working memory, but not the same thing. Short-term memory retains information while working memory retains *and* manipulates it.

One of the most well-known theories of working memory came from neuroscientists Alan Baddeley and Graham Hitch.[64] They proposed that working memory includes four components. The diagram below illustrates their perspective. For simplicity, I've pictured the four components as a conductor, an eye, an ear plus mouth, and a cement mixer). I explain each in the section that follows.

---

[61] "Stages of Memory - Sensory, Short-Term, Long-Term," accessed October 17, 2019, http://thepeakperformancecenter.com/educational-learning/learning/memory/stages-of-memory/.

[62] Sousa, p. 122.

[63] Sam Goldstein and Jack A. Naglieri, eds., *Handbook of Executive Functioning*, 2014 edition (Springer, 2013).

[64] Alan D. Baddeley and Graham Hitch, "Working Memory," in *Psychology of Learning and Motivation*, ed. Gordon H. Bower, vol. 8 (Academic Press, 1974), 47–89, https://doi.org/10.1016/S0079-7421(08)60452-1.

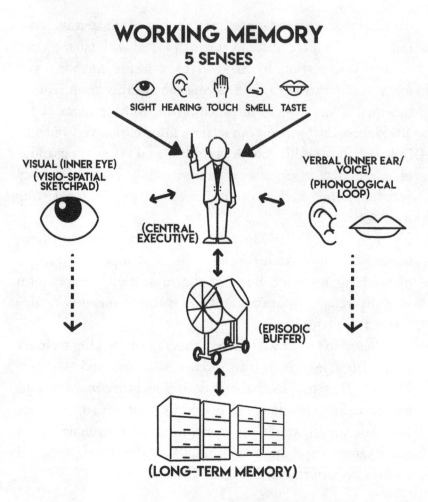

WORKING MEMORY
5 SENSES

SIGHT HEARING TOUCH SMELL TASTE

VISUAL (INNER EYE)
(VISIO-SPATIAL
SKETCHPAD)

(CENTRAL
EXECUTIVE)

VERBAL (INNER EAR/
VOICE)
(PHONOLOGICAL
LOOP)

(EPISODIC
BUFFER)

(LONG-TERM MEMORY)

Much of the information we receive comes from our five senses, pictured at the top part of the diagram. On the right side of the diagram, the inner ear/voice (called the phonological loop) relates to holding words in memory in a sound-based format. It's where we temporarily store language sounds It's called a loop because we can mentally rehearse sounds of words in a loop that lasts about two seconds. We can rehearse words out loud (vocalizing) or in our minds (called sub-vocalizing).

On the left side of the diagram, the inner eye (called the visuospatial sketchpad) is devoted to temporally storing visuospatial information. If you look around and then close your eyes, what you briefly see is what your sketchpad temporarily stored. Information gets there either by sensation (objectively what our senses tell us, the brain's bottom-up process), perception (how we subjectively interpret what our senses tell us, the brain's top-down process), or by retrieving information from long-term memory. In general, we sense from the bottom up and make sense of things from the top down.

Right now, I can think of and visualize my best childhood friend Bruce, but unless I keep my attention there, his image fades from consciousness. So, information arrives here via physically seeing something or via retrieving a memory from long-term memory.

Pictured in the upper center of the diagram is the conductor (called the central executive). The central executive works like a conductor guiding all of the instruments in an orchestra to work together in harmony, like a traffic cop coordinating traffic at an intersection, or even like a CEO coordinating a company's business activities. It delegates responsibilities to specific mental processes, monitors how well our mental processes are working, and makes sure we are moving toward our goals. As the central executive (conductor) coordinates things, both the phonological loop (the inner ear/voice) and the visuospatial sketchpad (inner eye) can work somewhat simultaneously.

For example, you can sketch a simple picture of a dog from memory. Your visuospatial sketchpad reaches into long-term memory to retrieve and then hold that image as you draw it. At the same time, you can quote a Scripture you've memorized (out loud or in your mind) which uses your phonological loop that has also drawn the memory trace of that particular

Scripture from long-term memory. Go ahead and try it. Your sketchpad allowed you to bring from long-term memory an image of a dog while your loop allowed you to retrieve and rehearse the verse, all at the same time.

Later, Baddeley added a fourth component called the episodic buffer, illustrated as a concrete mixer in the diagram. This part of working memory combines information from the central executive (the conductor) and from long-term memory. It also stores personal life episodes. Here, everything comes together, sometimes called *binding*. It connects working memory to long-term memory. It is limited in capacity and can store four chunks of information, plus or minus two. At one time, this limit was thought to be seven (plus or minus one) items called the "magical number seven"[65] (that's why our phone numbers are seven digits). Current research, however, indicates it's less. Baddeley describes the episodic buffer as, "a passive monitor that plays a multidimensional show, a show that has been prepared for us elsewhere in the brain and then projected on the monitor."[66]

Long-Term Memory

Our long-term memory has a very large storage capacity, equivalent to storing three million one-hour TV shows.[67] Retrieval from and transfer to long-term memory happens constantly between it and working memory. And memories

---

[65] Nelson Cowan, "The Magical Number 4 in Short-Term Memory: A Reconsideration of Mental Storage Capacity," *Behavioral and Brain Sciences* 24, no. 1 (February 2001): 87–114, https://doi.org/10.1017/S0140525X01003922.

[66] Østby, p. 173.

[67] Paul Reber, "What Is the Memory Capacity of the Human Brain?," *Scientific American*, accessed October 17, 2019, https://doi.org/10.1038/scientificamericanmind0510-70.

are stored in the same area of the brain where they were originally processed from sensory input.

For example, when you pick up a banana from the fruit basket on your table and eat it, several areas of your brain process that information. At the very back of your brain, your occipital lobe processes the color of the banana. Your parietal lobe, at the top of your brain, processes other information, including your sense of touch. Smell gets processed deep in your brain in the insula. Other aspects like size and shape also get processed in other areas and so on. So, the next time you reach for and eat a banana, memories from those same parts of the brain are reactivated to simultaneously get bound together in working memory, with the help of the hippocampus, to create the experience of eating a banana. How that happens is somewhat of a mystery, and it's called the *binding problem*.

So, how do memories get stored in long-term memory? The answer lies in a concept crucial to learning called memory consolidation, which the hippocampus helps do. Henry Molison (see the prior chapter) had both of his hippocampi removed which permanently kept his brain from forming new memories, although his working memory remained intact. The hippocampus consolidates or hardens memories in long-term memory, but it takes time for consolidation to occur. As consolidation happens gradually, it benefits our memory because we can incorporate new information without over-writing existing memories[68] and recall material more easily as a result. The hippocampus not only sends those memories

---

[68] James L. McClelland, Bruce L. McNaughton, and Randall C. O'Reilly, "Why There Are Complementary Learning Systems in the Hippocampus and Neocortex: Insights from the Successes and Failures of Connectionist Models of Learning and Memory.," *Psychological Review* 102, no. 3 (1994): 419–57, https://doi.org/10.1037/0033-295X.102.3.419.

to various places in the brain, but it is also involved in reactivating those brain memories to help recall a memory.

My daughter Tiffany suffered from mild seizures called absence seizures. She'd stare off into the distance for a few minutes. She'd be "absent." When she'd have a seizure, her hippocampus faced a firestorm of electrical activity. As a result, no consolidation occurred. She could not recall any memories from a few hours to days prior to her seizure. Gratefully, once the surgeon removed her right temporal lobe, the seizures stopped which helped her remember things better.

Initially, the hippocampus acts like a master organizer, "that gets all the relevant [brain] regions together to regenerate the visual, auditory, and tactile experiences associated with a particular memory. But over time, those … regions begin to communicate directly with each other and no longer need the hippocampus to get them together."[69] So over time (days and sometimes years), the memory is *hardened* enough in other parts of the brain so the hippocampus is no longer needed to reactivate and recall that memory. Research has discovered that if someone's hippocampus gets damaged, the person can often remember childhood memories, but not necessarily recent memories, up to three years prior. Before such an injury, those memories didn't have sufficient time to consolidate without needing the hippocampus to initiate retrieval.

So, retrievable memories end up in long-term memory when they've gone through four stages: encoding (acquiring them), consolidating (hardening them), storing (putting them somewhere), and retrieving (finding them when you want them).[70]

[69] Polk, *The Learning Brain*, The Great Courses (Chantilly, VA: The Great Courses, 2018), p. 22,
[70] Karim Nader and Oliver Hardt, "A Single Standard for Memory: The Case for Reconsolidation," *Nature Reviews. Neuroscience* 10, no. 3 (March 2009): 224–34, https://doi.org/10.1038/nrn2590.

And just because information makes it through the first stage of encoding, it does not guarantee that it can be recalled later. It must be retrieved, reactivated, and reconsolidated.[71]

Durable learning requires that the brain reactivates a pattern similar to the one that was activated in the first place, but with a different stimulus.[72] That is, real learning occurs when your learner can recall what you said in a context different from the classroom, boardroom, or church building where they learned it. Cues, mood, and context all affect retrieval (more on that later).[73] And this process is a whole brain activity with encoding involving more of the brain's left hemisphere and retrieval involving more of the brain's right hemisphere.[74]

It's important to note that the act of recalling a memory actually changes that memory. Each time we recall an episode in our lives, it's not as if the memory is an exact playback like a scene on a DVD that we can simply replay. Rather, each recall reconsolidates the memory and slightly alters it by adding or deleting some material. "Every time a memory is activated, it is altered."[75] That's why the memory of an eyewitness to a crime can be manipulated. This idea is also behind "false memories," memories of an event that never really happened

---

[71] Susan J. Sara, "Retrieval and Reconsolidation: Toward a Neurobiology of Remembering," *Learning & Memory* 7, no. 2 (January 3, 2000): 73–84, https://doi.org/10.1101/lm.7.2.73.

[72] Susumu Tonegawa, Mark D. Morrissey, and Takashi Kitamura, "The Role of Engram Cells in the Systems Consolidation of Memory," *Nature Reviews Neuroscience* 19, no. 8 (August 2018): 485–98, https://doi.org/10.1038/s41583-018-0031-2.

[73] Sousa, p. 123.

[74] Sousa, p. 122.

[75] Yana Weinstein, Megan Sumeracki, and Oliver Caviglioli, *Understanding How We Learn: A Visual Guide*, 1 edition (London; New York, NY: Routledge, 2018), p. 67.

but were confabulated—made up through the influence of another's input.

Some Forgetting Is Necessary

Theoretically, our brains probably have the capacity to store every experience in life. Although as I mentioned above, our brain can store data equal to three million one-hour TV shows,[76] which would take you 300 years to watch them all if that's all you did 24-7. But we don't want to remember everything. Forgetting can be good. During the daytime, our brain is in "record" mode, and at night, it switches to "edit" mode, editing out memories we don't need as it prunes neuronal connections and firms up the ones we do need (consolidation).

Forgetting is necessary for remembering. One researcher noted, "The ability to retrieve and generate information that is wanted, relevant, and appropriate is made possible by the ability to inhibit, and thus forget, information that is unwanted, irrelevant, and inappropriate … the ability to forget, at least under certain conditions, appears to reflect the adaptive functioning of memory, not its failure. As frustrating as forgetting might seem, we are far better with it than we would be without it."[77]

---

[76] Paul Reber, "What Is the Memory Capacity of the Human Brain?" *Scientific American*, accessed December 13, 2019, https://doi.org/10.1038/scientificamericanmind0510-70.

[77] Benjamin C. Storm, "The Benefit of Forgetting in Thinking and Remembering," *Current Directions in Psychological Science* 20, no. 5 (2011): 291–95.

Christianity and Memory

God does not bypass our memory to spiritually transform us. Granted, sometimes God uses miraculous means to communicate His truth. Many Muslims have believed in Jesus through dreams.[78] But He usually uses laws of His created order to get spiritual truth into our minds and hearts (i.e., sound waves generated by a teacher and our hearing mechanism that turns them into electrical impulses in our brains), and He uses people who create those sound waves, the communicators.

In ancient Judaism, memory was very important. Scholar Birger Gerhardsson writes, "Throughout his life, from birth to death, the Jew was surrounded by an endless succession of sign and symbol, ceaselessly exhorting him 'to remember'."[79]

Repetition was the primary tool for learning with the goal to memorize. Even today, repetition is key to learning. It provides the basic skills and understanding upon which to build more complex learning, it reduces forgetting, and it improves transfer to other life situations.[80] Practice makes permanent. In fact, in ancient history, some Jews demonstrated such extraordinary power to memorize that they became like living textbooks. When a rabbi in a more advanced learning environment needed to present some oral material to his students, he would call on these memory masters, called *tannaim*.[81] Unfortunately, memory today has

---

[78] Sam Martyn, "The Role of Pre-Conversion Dreams and Visions in Islamic Contexts: An Examination of the Evidence," *Southeastern Theological Review* 9, no. 2 (January 1, 2018): 55.

[79] Gerhardsson and Neusner, p 73.

[80] Willingham, *Why Students Don't Like School*, p. 1.

[81] Gerhardsson and Neusner, p. 99.

been essentially downloaded to textbooks. We have experienced the "dethronement of memory."[82]

The Jewish traditions were passed down, primarily orally, with the help of signs and symbols everywhere—in the home, the synagogue, schools, and the courts. In the early Jewish commentaries, called midrashim, they note, "The continuous experience ... is one of hearing, internalizing through repetition, and re-articulation, all the hallmarks of oral teaching."[83] And educational changes in the early Christian era, which patterned the Jewish systems, did not change for some time. The influence from modern educational innovations and patterns were long in coming.[84]

Historian Ian J. Shaw writes, "The command to remember is strong throughout Scripture. In Joshua 4, the Israelites were told to build a monument from stones that had been in the middle of the River Jordan to provoke the question from passers-by, 'What do these stones mean?' Then the history of the miraculous crossing of the Jordan would be retold. The Gospel writers reveal that Jesus often repeated His sayings. And Christians recall the words, 'Do this in remembrance of me,' when we observe the Lord's Supper. Remembrance is designed to feed faith. The Psalmist wrote, 'We have heard with our ears, O God; our fathers have told us what you did in their days, in days long ago' (Psalm 44:1)."[85]

So, it behooves us communicators to understand and apply how memory works when we prepare and deliver our talks to

---

[82] Nathan Morris, *The Jewish School*, 1st Edition (Eyre and Spottiswoode, 1937), p. 114.

[83] Steven D. Fraade, "Literary Composition and Oral Performance in Early Midrashim," *Oral Tradition*, 1999, http://citeseerx.ist.psu.edu/viewdoc/download?doi=10.1.1.502.6194&rep=rep1&type=pdf, pp. 33-34.

[84] Gerhardsson and Neusner, p. 77.

[85] Ian J. Shaw, *Christianity: The Biography: 2000 Years of Global History* (Zondervan Academic, 2017), p. 11.

our learners. In the next eight chapters, I will unpack the eight core principles along with three key practices for each.

* * *

APPLICATION

1. Why would understanding how memory works help you craft and deliver your talks better?
2. In your own words, distinguish the difference between sensory, working/short-term memory, and long-term memory.
3. Recall from memory the four parts of working memory, and explain each in your own words. This is an example of using cues to jog our memory.

Cen_____ _____ (conductor)
Vis_____ _____ (inner eye)
Phon_____ _____ (inner ear/voice)
Episo_____ _____ (mixer)

Check out the website for downloadable tools at
www.charlesstone.com/TEDfreebies

4

Principle One: Clarity ... Begin with the End in Mind

Everything should be made as simple as possible, but not simpler.   —Albert Einstein

Chapter Big Idea: Principle One—*Clarity ... Begin with the End in Mind* answers the question, *Where do you want to take your learners?* Three key practices will help you apply this principle:

1. Clarify the main take-away.
2. Create a concept map.
3. Capitalize on the primacy/recency memory bias.

I wrote this chapter in 2020 as election season in the U.S. was heating up. Various candidates vied for maximum TV exposure, so if a talk show invited them on, they usually jumped at the opportunity. As I surfed the net one day, I noticed a short video of a well-known candidate responding to questions on a talk show. The talk show panelists threw softball questions to the candidate and were overly gracious.

However, as I watched this candidate attempt to answer their questions, he could not articulate a clear answer. He mumbled a few unrelated phrases that made no sense. The panelists even tried to put words in his mouth to help him along, but he still could not put together a coherent, clear, thoughtful answer. Throughout that particular election cycle, this politician began to get the reputation as one who lacked the mental acuity necessary for the position he aspired, all related to his inability to clearly communicate.

This example is an extreme one, but it reminds us how important clarity is to communicators. In this chapter, I delve into the first principle, *Clarity—Begin with the End in Mind*. Clarity requires that you know where you want to take your learners.

* * *

PRACTICE ONE: CLARIFY THE BIG TAKEAWAY

Jesus often experienced tension with the religious elite of the day—the Scribes, Pharisees, and Sadducees. They approached faith in God from a pure behaviorist approach. Follow the law. Do what we tell you to do. Focus on prescribed behavior. Say the right prayers. Quote the right Scripture. Follow the right traditions.

Of course, Jesus believed in the Scriptures, prayer, and obedience. He fulfilled the law perfectly. He knew the Scriptures well, and He constantly prayed and communed with His Father. He wanted His followers to follow Him (which implied right behavior), but to do so from their hearts.

His ultimate goal for His followers was a transformed heart, a change in conduct and character that flowed from their soul. He sought to reshape intentions, motivations, inclinations, thoughts, and actions. Jesus often contrasted His teaching with the teaching from the religious establishment with, "You have heard that it was said, but *I* tell you … (Matt. 5)." His way was different.

Jesus knew His overarching purpose was to do His Father's will (John 4:34), and He knew what He needed to say to the masses. He was clear about His goal for His followers— that they become like Him. He said, "A student is not above his teacher, but everyone who is fully trained will be like his teacher (Luke 6:40)." Jesus began His ministry with the end in mind—to do His Father's will. And in doing so, people's hearts would be transformed. As they became His followers, they would become salt and light and fishers of men.

Jesus never lacked clarity about His mission, and His teaching reflected that clarity. We communicators must also be clear about where we want to take our learners. It's crucial to clarify your talk's main idea or big takeaway as you begin to craft your talk. One helpful way to do that is to frame your talk and your main idea as an answer to questions like one of these:

Why should your learners want to listen to you (the "*What's in it for me?*" question)?

What is the central question you want to answer for your listeners or the problem you want to help them solve?

What do your learners need to know to answer the question or solve the problem?

If your learners could only remember one idea, what would it be?

How clear are you on what you hope they will do with what you say?

The Throughline

Every screenwriter writes a movie or TV show script around a clear "throughline." It's like an imaginary chord that connects the various scenes and components of the movie or show, a "connecting theme that ties together each narrative element."[86] View your big takeaway in your talk like a throughline to connect all of your points, ideas, and illustrations. One way to view your throughline is to see it (your big idea) like the trunk of a tree. All of your points, illustrations, and explanations would then be like the branches attached to the trunk.

You'll want to summarize your throughline in a single sentence of less than 15 words which clearly states what you want your audience to take away. TED Talks garner millions of viewers, partly because the organizers expect every presenter to craft a clear and compelling throughline.[87] When your audience knows where you want to take them, they're more likely to follow. Developing a clear throughline implies that you must "plan backwards." That is, you must first decide what you want your learners to take away and then develop your talk based on that. However, don't confuse a throughline with a title. A throughline gives more meat than what a title

---

86 Anderson, p. 30.
87 Anderson, p. 30.

might convey. Let's say you're speaking on biblical love. A title might be, *Love: the Greatest Force in the World*. A throughline might be, *We experience the power of love when we allow the love of Christ to flow through us.*

Gist or Verbatim?

In her book, *Impossible to Ignore*, double PhD scientist Dr. Carmen Simon describes another perspective of memory—gist memory and verbatim memory. Gist memory relates to the general meaning of something we recall and is less specific than verbatim memory which is more word-for-word recall. Gist memories tend to last longer, and if you aim your talk toward gist memory, you can get away with giving more content. Our learners' attention will wax and wane when we speak. When their internal dialogue is more rewarding and valuable than our words at that moment, the brain releases stronger brain chemicals which strengthens gist memory around the meaning they are making during those moments of reflection.[88]

So, when you develop your main takeaway (throughline), ask yourself which kind of memory you want to evoke, gist or verbatim. As Dr. Simon writes, "Do you want people to remember exactly what you say or … sort of what you say?"[89] The kind of memory you hope to evoke can help guide you as you craft your main idea and choose appropriate communication tools for your talk. Your intended audience will also influence this decision whether you choose gist, verbatim, or a combination of the two. If you are speaking to a group of

---

[88] Carmen Simon, *Impossible to Ignore: Creating Memorable Content to Influence Decisions*, 1 edition (New York: McGraw-Hill Education, 2016), Kindle e-book loc. 749-759.

[89] Simon, Kindle e-book loc. 777.

scientists, you may want to target verbatim memory. If you're trying to connect to your youth group, you may want to target gist memory. *When* you want your leaners to act upon what you say will also help you decide. If you want them to quickly act upon what you say, choose verbatim memory. If want them to act later, choose gist memory since it lasts longer.

Although I devote a future chapter to how emotions enhance learning, it's helpful to understand now how emotion impacts gist and verbatim memory. Neuroscientist Dr. John Medina writes these helpful words:

> The brain remembers the emotional components of an experience better than any other aspect. We might forget minute details of an interstate fender bender, for example, yet vividly recall the fear of trying to get to the shoulder without further mishap. Studies show that emotional arousal focuses attention on the "gist" of an experience at the expense of peripheral details. Many researchers think that's how memory normally works—by recording the gist of what we encounter, not by retaining a literal record of the experience. With the passage of time, our retrieval of gist always trumps our recall of details.[90]

One way to clarify gist is to ask yourself what 10% of your talk do you hope your learners will recall and then reinforce that information in your talk.

---

[90] John Medina, *Brain Rules: 12 Principles for Surviving and Thriving at Work, Home, and School*, Reprint (Pear Press, 2009), Kindle e-book loc. 1196.

The 5 Cs

Effective writers use a template called the 5 Cs when they write. Each "C" relates to a specific writing goal. In addition to the throughline and gist or verbatim memory, consider the 5 Cs to help clarify your big takeaway:

o Clear—Use simple, clear words without trying to impress your learner with your vocabulary.

o Concise—Use less than 15 words.

o Compelling—Use colorful words; writing instructors often say, "Show, don't tell."

o Catalytic—Make it motivational and aspirational.

o Contextual—Keep it within the context of your intended audience.

* * *

PRACTICE TWO: CREATE A CONCEPT MAP

In the prior chapter, I referred to pre-encoding and the idea of, "tell 'em what you're going to tell 'em and then tell 'em." I originally learned that idea from a preaching class in seminary. The first part of the phrase, "Tell 'em what you're gonna tell 'em," relates to a key idea that will enhance your communication. It's called a concept map, a visual way to pre-encode through an outline or visual summary of your talk's main concepts. It's a tool that provides scaffolding to help learners learn more and better. Just as physical scaffolding helps a brick layer get higher up, learning scaffolding, like a concept map, helps listeners get "higher up" in their understanding from your talk and facilitates the "transfer" of their knowledge to other areas, or in other words, application.[91] It helps learners see the big picture and how all the pieces fit together in meaningful ways.

My dad loves jigsaw puzzles. When he gets a new puzzle, he performs the same routine each time. He takes the pieces out and puts them on a table. He then turns them over to the printed side, stands the box on end so he sees the overall picture, looks for all the pieces with a straight edge to create the border, and then fills in the puzzle. Imagine if he had no picture to look at. He'd never put the puzzle together. A concept map is like the jigsaw puzzle's picture on the box and like the border. It gives meaning, overall structure, and the big picture.

God designed our brain to look for patterns.[92] A concept map, through graphically organizing the material, helps a learner see those patterns. It guides them to connect new learning to prior learning and helps them see connections to your overall objectives (the patterns), thus enhancing learning.[93] A concept map can help your learners see the big picture, connect prior knowledge to current knowledge, and see the overarching structure and broad objectives you will address in your talk.

Research shows that concept maps significantly improve student's learning in contrast to a lecture with no concept

---

[91] Matthew T. McCrudden, Gregory Schraw, and Stephen Lehman, "The Use of Adjunct Displays to Facilitate Comprehension of Causal Relationships in Expository Text," *Instructional Science* 37, no. 1 (2009): 65–86, https://doi.org/10.1007/s11251-007-9036-3.

[92] Arkady Konovalov, Ian Krajbich. *Neurocomputational Dynamics of Sequence Learning. Neuron*, 2018; DOI: 10.1016/j.neuron.2018.05.013.

[93] Chei-Chang Chiou, "The Effect of Concept Mapping on Students' Learning Achievements and Interests," *Innovations in Education & Teaching International* 45 (November 1, 2008), https://doi.org/10.1080/14703290802377240.

map.[94] Concept maps help a learner clarify, understand, and integrate their learning, and it enhances their interest in what you have to say.[95] At the basic brain level, concept maps work because they tap into the way our brains process information. The brain first processes overall meaning or gist before it processes detail.[96] So, a concept map that includes your overall big ideas will reinforce how your learner's brain naturally works which will deepen their learning.[97, 98]

Concept maps also free up working memory.[99] When you provide concepts in an external visible form, you allow them to make the connections outside their head. As a result, they gain access to more working memory to use on other higher-level tasks like forming other connections to your basic ideas. That helps them progress faster than they would have otherwise.

One final benefit from a concept map, a cheat sheet of sorts, gives them a quick way to review what they've learned.

---

[94] Mine Taşkin et al., "The Effect of Concept Maps in Teaching Sportive Technique," *Procedia - Social and Behavioral Sciences*, Teachers for the Knowledge Society, 11 (January 1, 2011): 141–44, https://doi.org/10.1016/j.sbspro.2011.01.049.

[95] Chiou, "The Effect of Concept Mapping on Students' Learning Achievements and Interests."

[96] John Medina, *Brain Rules: 12 Principles for Surviving and Thriving at Work, Home, and School*, Reprint (Pear Press, 2009), Kindle e-book loc. 1200.

[97] Jerry Chih-Yuan Sun and Ariel Yu-Zhen Chen, "Effects of Integrating Dynamic Concept Maps with Interactive Response System on Elementary School Students' Motivation and Learning Outcome: The Case of Anti-Phishing Education," *Computers & Education* 102 (November 1, 2016): 117–27, https://doi.org/10.1016/j.compedu.2016.08.002.

[98] Chiou, "The Effect of Concept Mapping on Students' Learning Achievements and Interests."

[99] Bonnie D. Singer and Anthony S. Bashir, "Wait. . . What??? Guiding Intervention Principles for Students With Verbal Working Memory Limitations," *Language, Speech & Hearing Services in Schools* 49, no. 3 (July 2018): 449–62, https://doi.org/10.1044/2018_LSHSS-17-0101.

And for those who express their ideas through art, visualizing or even drawing connections between the big picture and other ideas can be fun and effective for them.[100]

So, what might a concept map look like? It might be a vertical org chart with main points inside connected boxes or circles that point up to the main idea. It might look like a mind map with the main idea in the middle and lines going out to other boxes or circles that include sub-ideas. It might take the form of a few pictures or simple symbols that visualize your main idea and points. It could be a slide with the main point at the top with bullet points below it that briefly describe your sub ideas. For more concept map ideas, you can download some free examples from the website at www.charlesstone.com/TEDfreebies.

Finally, if you want to supercharge the benefit from a concept map, give your learners the task to create their own maps after you've shared yours. Learning will deepen further still.[101]

Jesus often used a version of concept maps when He prefaced a word picture with this phrase: *the kingdom of God is like* .... He created an image in the listener's minds about the Kingdom with what followed this phrase. He used visuals such as a farmer sowing seed (Matt. 13:24), a mustard seed (Matt. 13:31), leaven (Matt. 13:33), a treasure (Matt. 13:44), pearls (Matt. 13:45), a fishnet (Matt. 13:47), a king (Matt. 18:23), and a landowner (Matt. 20:1). These visuals served as a type of concept map to set the listener up for the lesson that followed.

---

[100] Singer and Bashir.

[101] Marije Amelsvoort, Jerry Andriessen, and G. Kanselaar, "How Students Structure and Relate Argumentative Knowledge When Learning Together with Diagrams," *Computers in Human Behavior* 24 (May 1, 2008): 1293–1313, https://doi.org/10.1016/j.chb.2007.05.004.

* * *

PRACTICE THREE:
CAPITALIZE ON THE PRIMACY/
RECENCY MEMORY BIAS

The primacy/recency effect bias means that in a talk, we best remember what comes first and remember what comes last second best. Educational expert David Sousa explains it this way:

The first items of new information are within the working memory's functional capacity, so they command our attention and are likely to be retained in semantic memory [long-term memory related to our capacity to remember words, concepts, or numbers]. The later information, however, exceeds the capacity and is lost. As the learning episode concludes, items in working memory are sorted or chunked to allow for additional processing of the arriving final items, which are likely held in working memory and will decay unless further rehearsed.[102]

This is what he means. Imagine our working memory like a small chalkboard. When what we write fills it up, there is no room to write more. In a similar fashion, our learner's mental chalkboard tends to fill up at the beginning of a talk and new information has nowhere to go. The brain needs time to process and send it to long-term memory which means less new information enters working memory. That's why what we say in the middle of a talk is not remembered as well. As Sousa

---

[102] Sousa, p. 100.

notes above, during the middle part of your talk, the brain updates long-term memory and chunks the new material so that more working memory becomes available toward the end of your talk.

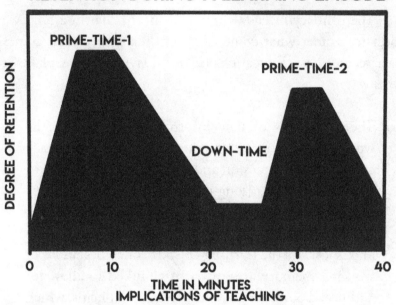

RETENTION DURING A LEARNING EPISODE

IMPLICATIONS OF TEACHING

This is an important concept for communicators to keep in mind. Teach your new and most important material first and then revisit it toward the end. Ideally, you can break up your talk into sections to give a brain break between each one. And keep in mind that the longer your talk goes, as more information accumulates more can *fall off* their mental chalkboard. This cluttering can interfere with the sorting and chunking process, increase forgetting, and thus hinder learning.[103] However, this concept does not mean that short is always good. Short may feel good, but it doesn't necessarily foster durable learning. You can foster durable learning in a longer presentation when you apply the principles I've explained in this book.

* * *

So in summary, *Principle One: Clarity—Begin with the End in Mind* means that when you create your talk, you'll want work backwards from the end goal. The following three practices support this principle. First, clarify your big take-away by keeping in mind the throughline, gist or verbatim memory goal, and the 5 Cs of good writing (and communicating). Second, create a concept map to visually picture what you're going to say. Finally, remember the primacy/recency memory bias. Your learners best remember the first ideas you share and remember your last ideas second best. Place the most important concepts toward the beginning and the end of your talk.

---

[103] Gemma. Elliott, Claire L. Isaac, and Nils Muhlert, "Measuring Forgetting: A Critical Review of Accelerated Long-Term Forgetting Studies," *Cortex; a Journal Devoted to the Study of the Nervous System and Behavior* 54, no. 100 (May 2014): 16–32, https://doi.org/10.1016/j.cortex.2014.02.001.

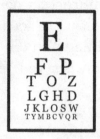

**Principle One: CLARITY—
BEGIN WITH THE END IN MIND**

Where do you want to take your learners?

o   Clarify the big takeaway(s): gist or verbatim memory, the "10%".
o   Create a concept map.
o   Capitalize on the primacy/recency principle.

In the next chapter we'll look at *Principle Two: Attention— Pique Interest.*

* * *

APPLICATION

1. Look at the last talk you gave. Ask yourself how clear you were on where you wanted to take your learners. Was your big idea clear? If it wasn't, write out one that would fit.
2. In your own words, define a concept map. Draw out a concept map for the talk from application point one above.
3. In your own words, define the primacy/recency memory bias. How well did your recent talk incorporate the concept? How would you re-order your material to reflect the concept were you to give it again?

Check out the website for downloadable tools at
www.charlesstone.com/TEDfreebies

5

Principle Two: Attention ...
Pique Interest

Attention is a limited resource, so pay attention to where you pay attention. —Howard Rheingold

Whatever you focus your attention on will become important to you, even if it's unimportant.
—Sonya Parker

Chapter Big Idea: Principle One—*Attention ... Pique Interest* answers the question, *How can you get your listeners to listen?* Three key practices will help you apply this principle.

1. Adapt your talk to the dynamics of attention.
2. Add appropriate attention grabbers.
3. Apply priming.

In 2015, the pages of *Time, USA, The Guardian,* and other magazines prominently displayed this headline: **You Now have a Shorter Attention Span than a Goldfish.**[104] It quoted a study for Microsoft by Canadian researchers who surveyed 2,000 people and studied the brain activity of 112 others using EEG. The article stated researchers discovered that since 2000, the average human attention span had dropped from twelve seconds to eight seconds. Your kids' goldfish apparently maintains attention longer, nine seconds. That story with the catchy goldfish anecdote swept through the internet, and it still persists today.

The only problem? It was false. The eight-second figure was actually taken from another website that could not back up their eight-second claim with *any* research.[105] Eight seconds actually reflected the average time a person spent on a webpage before moving to another one.[106]

This neuromyth highlights the interest and attention we pay to … attention. Another neuromyth considered common knowledge is that attention from students during a lecture lasts only 10-15 minutes. This also lacks evidence-based research to support it. The neuromyth has been propagated by many who relied on a 1978 literature review on how the amount of note-taking declined during a lecture after 10-15 minutes.[107] They

[104] Kevin McSpadden, "You Now Have a Shorter Attention Span Than a Goldfish," Time, accessed March 21, 2020, https://time.com/3858309/attention-spans-goldfish/.
[105] Simon Maybin, "Busting the Attention Span Myth," *BBC News*, March 10, 2017, sec. Health, https://www.bbc.com/news/health-38896790.
[106] Neil A. Bradbury, "Attention Span during Lectures: 8 Seconds, 10 Minutes, or More?," *Advances in Physiology Education* 40, no. 4 (December 1, 2016): 509–13, https://doi.org/10.1152/advan.00109.2016.
[107] James Hartley and Ivor K. Davies, "Note-taking: A Critical Review," *Programmed Learning and Educational Technology* 15, no. 3 (August 1, 1978): 207–24, https://doi.org/10.1080/0033039780150305.

concluded that notetaking declined not because attention waned but because lecture content dropped and the decline does not necessarily indicate a decline in attention. Yet, this neuromyth also persists.

Although such neuromyths never seem to die, our ability to maintain attention does appear to be waning in today's 24/7, always-on culture. Psychologists have even coined a term to describe a problem that afflicts 30-40% of the workforce—attention deficit trait, ADT.[108]

Attention has captured the interest of many through the ages. William James, considered the founder of modern psychology, once noted, "The faculty of voluntarily bringing back a wandering attention, over and over again, is the very root of judgment, character, and will."[109] When I refer to attention, I'm referring to "all the mechanisms by which the brain selects information, amplifies it, channels it, and deepens its processing."[110]

God gave us the ability to pay attention and select where we put it because our brains can't process everything our senses perceive from our environment. We simply cannot digest it all. And the Scriptures remind us genuine faith that effects spiritual transformation requires hearing which requires attention (Rom. 10:17). So, we might also say that hearts can't be transformed without attention.

Jesus commanded people's attention and would often arrest their attention with different phrases. He said, "I tell you" (in numerous Scriptures), "He who has ears to hear

---

[108] Alorie Gilbert, "Why Can't You Pay Attention Anymore? - CNET News," CNET, March 28, 2005, http://news.cnet.com/Why-cant-you-pay-attention-anymore/2100-1022_3-5637632.html.
[109] William James, Psychology: Briefer Course, (Harper Torchbooks, 1961), p. 424.
[110] Dehaene, p. 147.

let him hear" (Mark 4:9, 23; Luke 14:35), and, "Listen and understand" (Matt. 15:10). Sometimes, He would even ask them if they understood (Matt. 16:9, 24:43; Mark 4:13). He was so effective at keeping attention that it sometimes created problems for Him. Mark records one time He captured people's attention so well that crowds grew so large and crowded around Him that He had to use a boat as a temporary platform (Mark 4:1). On another occasion, He kept the crowd's attention so effectively that they apparently forgot to eat (Mark 6:35-36).

So, it behooves us communicators to pay attention to attention because nothing gets learned that is not paid attention to. Paying little or no attention induces little or no learning.[111] Attention is necessary for retention but does not guarantee it. Attention provides one substantial piece of the learning puzzle, but not all of it. In the pages ahead, you'll learn about other cognitive puzzle pieces that contribute to durable learning.

* * *

PRACTICE ONE:
ADAPT YOUR TALK TO THE DYNAMICS OF ATTENTION

Every parent has probably told their child multiple times, "Pay attention to me!" Our attention simply wanders, whether we are a child or an adult. And durable learning depends on attention. The first few seconds in a talk are very important, as author and business coach Paul Hellman writes, "When you stand up and speak, your audience experiences you like a

---

[111] Dehaene, p. 148.

movie. Their first thought being, *Is this movie interesting?* And they may only give you eight seconds to find out."[112]

So, how does attention in our brains work?

Attention involves the ability to focus on something (like an amplifier) while ignoring distractions at the same time (like a filter). Dr. Mel Levine, author and child education expert, says that three types of control structures influence attention, "mental energy control (which decides one's level of alertness, the balance between sleep and wakefulness, and consistency in achievement), processing control (which decides what's important, as in saliency, and is responsible for detail processing), and production control (which determines orders and steps and is responsible for self-monitoring)."[113] Control as well as process influences attention. So, to pay attention means that we choose, filter, and select the object of our attention.

A popular evidence-based model that explains attention was originally developed by Dr. Michael Posner.[114] This model incorporates three distinct sequential brain processes or networks:

- An *alerting* network involving the brain stem arousal systems and the right hemisphere—the *when* to attend that increases our level of vigilance
- An *orienting* network involving the parietal cortex (on top of our brain)—the *what* to attend to that amplifies what we pay attention to

---

[112] Paul Hellman, *You've Got 8 Seconds: Communication Secrets for a Distracted World* (AMACOM, 2017), p. 93.

[113] Tokuhama-Espinosa, p. 122.

[114] Steven E. Petersen and Michael I. Posner, "The Attention System of the Human Brain: 20 Years After," *Annual Review of Neuroscience* 35 (July 21, 2012): 73–89, https://doi.org/10.1146/annurev-neuro-062111-150525.

- An *executive (or maintaining)* network involving the cingulate cortex (a bit behind our forehead) which "decides how to process the attended information, selects the processes that are relevant to a given task, and controls their execution"[115]

In the first phase, since our brain constantly scans our environment for something unusual, when something unusual does occur, it senses it and is alerted (the when). A brain chemical (neurotransmitter) called norepinephrine enhances this signal. In the orient phase, we seek more information by orienting our attention to it (the where). Acetylcholine, a neurotransmitter involved in learning, plays a role here. This neurotransmitter is strongly involved in the neural circuitry that enhances attention.[116] And in the final phase, we become conscious of the stimulus, respond to it, and focus our attention on it. Dopamine is involved in this phase as it helps block other distractions. This process can be compared to the three parts of firing a gun—load, aim, fire.

Another helpful metaphor for understanding attention is how spotlights are used in an auditorium during a theatrical performance. First, the lights go down (the producers gain your attention because the show is about to begin—the *alerting* stage). A spotlight then focuses on the main character on stage (they direct your attention—the *orienting* phase), and then the spotlight changes its focus to various key characters at different moments during the play (they sustain your attention where they want you to continue to place it—the *act* or *maintaining* phase).

---

[115] Dehaene, p. 150.

[116] Martin Sarter, William J. Gehring, and Rouba Kozak, "More Attention Must Be Paid: The Neurobiology of Attentional Effort," *Brain Research Reviews* 51, no. 2 (August 2006): 145–60, https://doi.org/10.1016/j.brainresrev.2005.11.002.

So, when you deliver your talk, all three of these components of attention come into play in your learners' brains: *listen* (gain their attention), listen to *this* (focus their attention), *keep* listening to this (maintain their attention). This sequence happens repeatedly in your listener's brain during every talk you give. Jesus masterfully gained and maintained His learners' attention.[117] He asked for it as He often said, "He who has ears to hear, let them hear (Mark 4:9), and the result was that the people, "hung on His words (Luke 19:48)."

As noted above, neurotransmitters (chemicals in our brain) play a role in attention. Too much or too little dopamine can inhibit attention. Acetylcholine affects brain processing speed, acting somewhat like a neural lubricant that keeps energy and information flowing well. A lack of it can create brain fog and inhibit attention. GABA is another neurotransmitter involved in learning and helps produce the feel-good hormones we experience in exercise and sex.[118] In addition, "Oxytocin makes our neuronal pathways more malleable, enabling us to learn—and unlearn—more readily than we normally would."[119]

Dopamine is worth further mention because it's one of the most crucial neurotransmitters involved in attention and learning. Learning feels good because dopamine is involved. When we help our listeners anticipate a future reward (we might say, *feel the future*), the brain gets a spritz of dopamine which can help them pay better attention, cement a memory

---

[117] Walter Albion Squires, *The Pedagogy of Jesus in The Twilight of To-Day*, First Edition (George H. Doran, 1927), pp. 84-89.

[118] Charles Stone, *Holy Noticing: The Bible, Your Brain, and the Mindful Space Between Moments* (Moody Publishers, 2019), p. 206.

[119] Friederike Fabritius and Hans W. Hagemann, *The Leading Brain: Powerful Science-Based Strategies for Achieving Peak Performance* (TarcherPerigee, 2017), p. 183.

or future cue, and feel motivated to take action.[120] When we learn something new and get that dopamine spritz, our brain wants to repeat that experience, resulting in motivation to learn more and repeat that activity.

In this case, the activity is learning. Our brain delivers dopamine through a collection of neurons called the dopaminergic system that projects into our thinking center, memory center, pleasure center, and motor control center. It also impacts certain brain mechanisms related to positive experiences that include wanting, liking, and learning.[121] Wanting gives us the motivation to do something. Liking gives us the pleasure of a behavior. Learning helps us remember what was pleasurable and predicts that a similar action in the future will give us more pleasure. Good communicators help create anticipation (and attention) in the learner for what is to come which causes their brain to release dopamine.

Another part of the brain called the reticular activating system (RAS) works like how shutters work on windows. Just as we can adjust how much sun we allow into a window by adjusting the shutters, the RAS does the same thing, only with attention. It allows only the most important stuff to get in and filters out the rest. All external stimuli (except smell) first flows through this system of neurons in our brain stem.

Finally, it's important for communicators to realize that attention is not a fixed constant. Rather, it varies from person to person and context to context. Each of your listeners has their own genetic attention capability based on many factors

[120] Arif A. Hamid et al., "Mesolimbic Dopamine Signals the Value of Work," *Nature Neuroscience* 19, no. 1 (January 2016): 117–26, https://doi.org/10.1038/nn.4173.
[121] Carmen Simon, *Impossible to Ignore: Creating Memorable Content to Influence Decisions*, 1 edition (New York: McGraw-Hill Education, 2016), Kindle e-book locs. 1476-1487.

like working memory, myelin (insulation around a neuron's tail that affects your brain's processing speed), lack of sleep, motivation, how much their mind wanders, boredom, and even nutrition.

Ubiquitous digital technologies have impacted attention, as one of the world's leading educational thinkers Dr. Daniel Willingham notes, "The consequence of long-term experience with digital technologies is not an inability to sustain attention. It's impatience with boredom. It's an expectation that I should always have something interesting to listen to, watch, or read, and that creating an interesting experience should require little effort. [...] We're not distractible. We just have a very low threshold for boredom."[122] Willingham observes that our digital world has degraded attention because we're bored. We communicators can also be guilty of degrading attention if we give boring talks.[123]

Although attention span is not the same for everyone, every listener will reach their personal threshold of attention at some point. When they cross it, learning will diminish because they focus less, encode less into their long-term memory, and thus retain less.[124] Your challenge is to design and deliver your talks with attention in mind so that you can maximize it.

* * *

---

[122] Daniel T. Willingham, *The Reading Mind: A Cognitive Approach to Understanding How the Mind Reads*, 1 edition (San Francisco, CA: Jossey-Bass, 2017), p. 173.

[123] James Farley, Evan Risko, and Alan Kingstone, "Everyday Attention and Lecture Retention: The Effects of Time, Fidgeting, and Mind Wandering," *Frontiers in Psychology* 4 (2013), https://doi.org/10.3389/fpsyg.2013.00619.

[124] Joshua R. Eyler, *How Humans Learn: The Science and Stories behind Effective College Teaching*, 1st edition (Morgantown: West Virginia University Press, 2018), p. 167.

PRACTICE TWO:
ADD APPROPRIATE ATTENTION GRABBERS
AND SUSTAINERS

Jesus understood how to capture and keep His learners' attention, and He masterfully used many techniques. He used metaphors (Matt. 5:15, John 7:38), similes (Matt. 4:30-32), hyperboles (Matt. 5:29), proverbs (John 15:20), irony (Mark 2:17), contrast (Matt. 6:19-20), puns (John 3:3), and even humor (Matt. 19:24, Luke 6:42). As He taught penetrating insights about difficult subjects, He did so in a way that was clear, straightforward, and attention arresting.

Sometimes, He used overstatement to grab their attention. For example, He said that to be a true disciple, you must hate your father and mother (Luke 14:26). He said you must pluck out your eye if it causes you to sin (Matt. 5:29-30). And He said you could move a mountain with faith as small as a mustard seed (Matt. 17:20). These gross overstatements captured the attention of the people.

He used enigmas (Matt. 24:28) and paradoxes (Luke 18:25) to maintain attention. He used these puzzling conundrums for several reasons.[125] Fundamentally, He wanted people to think for themselves. He also wanted to startle the smug (Matt. 19:12), rebuke the scoffer (Luke 17:20-21), or make a statement that would make sense later on (John 12:12-16).

As you plan your talk, think through the tools and techniques that could grab and sustain attention. You've only won a partial battle when your learners initially pay attention. That's often the easiest part. The hard work comes when you must sustain their attention.

---

[125] Robert G. Delnay, *Teach As He Taught: How to Apply Jesus' Teaching Methods* (Chicago: Moody Pub, 1987), p. 65.

Novelty and Curiosity

I suggest three attention grabbers in this section and primarily focus on novelty and curiosity—neural cousins.[126] Curiosity has been called the "wick in the candle of learning."[127] Although experts in the science of curiosity haven't arrived at a consensus definition, they generally agree it's one of the most powerful influencers of human behavior and learning.[128] Research shows that more curiosity leads to greater engagement with the material at hand which results in better learning.[129]

Our God-designed curiosity makes our brain pay attention to the novel. One of the foremost researchers on curiosity, George Lowenstein, defines curiosity as an "information gap," the distance between "what one knows and what one wants to know."[130] So, curiosity enhances learning as it acts like an engine of discovery.[131]

Since the brain is pattern seeking, curiosity drives the learner to make a prediction about a potential pattern. When you use novelty to engage the brain's innate curiosity, it aids recall and memory for this reason. When there is a promise of reward (the thing that piques curiosity, finding the pattern), "it creates a special encoding state in the hippocampus [a

---

[126] M. T. Bardo, R. L. Donohew, and N. G. Harrington, "Psychobiology of Novelty Seeking and Drug Seeking Behavior," *Behavioural Brain Research* 77, no. 1–2 (May 1996): 23–43, https://doi.org/10.1016/0166-4328(95)00203-0.

[127] Min Jeong Kang et al., "The Wick in the Candle of Learning: Epistemic Curiosity Activates Reward Circuitry and Enhances Memory," *Psychological Science* 20, no. 8 (August 2009): 963–73, https://doi.org/10.1111/j.1467-9280.2009.02402.x.

[128] Eyler, p. 19.

[129] Cavanagh, *The Spark of Learning*, p. 6.

[130] Eyler, p. 20.

[131] Eyler, p. 223.

part of the brain involved in memory] … which … heightens the release of dopamine,"[132] that important neurotransmitter involved in learning and reward. Dopamine increases when novelty and curiosity is high. And when dopamine increases in our brain's memory and pleasure centers, we simply learn better.[133] This process improves not only memory of the current material being learned but also material learned before and after the current material that has nothing to do with the current reward.

Educational experts McTighe and Willis write:

When learners are curious about something, they are in a perfect mental state to want to make predictions. Prediction activates the brain's instinctual need to know the result of one's choice, decision, action, or answer. When teachers provide opportunities for students to make predictions about the relationship of the curious sensory input or other novelty to the lesson, the students will seek information to help them make correct predictions, and they will remain attentive as the brain seeks to find out if the prediction is correct. Teachers can use "hooks"—such as a surprise, an anomaly, or a provocative question—to spark students' curiosity, setting the stage for having the students make predictions that will prompt their brains to attend to the lesson as it becomes a source of clues to guide or adjust their correct predictions.

---

[132] Alan Baddeley, Michael W. Eysenck, and Michael C. Anderson, *Memory*, 3 edition (Routledge, 2020), p. 154.

[133] Matthias J. Gruber, Bernard D. Gelman, and Charan Ranganath, "States of Curiosity Modulate Hippocampus-Dependent Learning via the Dopaminergic Circuit," *Neuron* 84, no. 2 (October 22, 2014): 486–96, https://doi.org/10.1016/j.neuron.2014.08.060.

After their curiosity is provoked, students will sustain attention if they are asked to predict what the curiosity-stimulating sight, sound, object, statement, picture, or question has to do with the lesson.[134]

In summary, "the more curious you are about something, the more likely you are to remember it."[135]

Jesus brought novelty into Jewish tradition when He accepted, valued, and honored women, because at the time, Judaism did not value women as highly as they did men. He modeled novelty when He loved the marginalized and oppressed, a practice that got Him into trouble with the religious elite. And He innovated Jewish law when He gave a new motive for the Sabbath and told His followers to love their enemies rather than getting even (i.e., an eye for an eye).

He used curiosity when He taught. "He produced in His disciples the mental condition needed for the presentation of important truths"[136]—curiosity. Once when He returned from a village, they were ready to eat, but Jesus sat apart and didn't join them. The disciples encourage Him to eat, but He responded with, "I have food to eat that you know nothing about (John 4:31-32." In moving, "from the concrete to the abstract, from the material to the spiritual,"[137] He set up a moment of curiosity in the disciples. He did the same in a conversation with a Samaritan woman at a well that's recorded

---

[134] Jay McTighe and Judy Willis, *Upgrade Your Teaching: Understanding by Design Meets Neuroscience* (Alexandria, Virginia: ASCD, 2019), Kindle e-book loc. 1899.

[135] Dehaene, *How We Learn*, p. 188.

[136] Naugle, "Information or Transformation? The Pedagogy of Jesus the Master Teacher and Its Implications."

[137] Naugle.

in John 4. "He aroused curiosity in every one of His first five sentences" in that encounter.[138]

Jesus often asked for His listeners' attention to pique their curiosity when He would ask them to *hear* (Matt. 11:15), *listen* (Matt. 13:18), or *behold* (Matt. 10:16, KJV). In one incident, Matthew records that a crowd of over 5,000 had gathered to hear Jesus speak and have Him heal their sick (Matt. 14:13-21). As evening approached, the disciples asked Jesus to dismiss the people so the crowd could find food in the local villages. Jesus then set up a curious dilemma for them when He responded, "They do not need to go away. You give them something to eat (verse 16)."

This perplexed the disciples because they only had five loaves of bread and two fish, enough to feed only a few. He further piqued their curiosity when He took what they had, directed the crowd to sit down, and thanked His Heavenly Father for the food, implying He was going to feed the massive crowd with a meager amount of food. I wish I could have been a fly on the wall to hear their conversations as Jesus did that. The disciples must have been riveted to Jesus' words and actions during this curiosity-creating miracle.

So, novelty and curiosity are powerful tools to create attention. However, novelty for novelty's sake won't enhance learning, and too much novelty can work against you if your listener can't connect the novel to the familiar. You'll want to strike a balance between the familiar and the novel—what to reveal and what to withhold. As Dr. Carmen Simon writes, "As a communicator, you must balance how much information to reveal (and allow listeners' brains to predict accurately) and how much information to withhold (and get listeners ready

[138] Robert G. Delnay, *Teach As He Taught: How to Apply Jesus' Teaching Methods* (Chicago: Moody Pub, 1987), p. 45.

for action, even if the action only implies people showing up to listen to you)."[139]

Novelty triggers our alerting system (listen) and orienting system (listen to this)[140] and thus grabs attention. However, novelty won't sustain attention (keep listening to this). Once you use something novel and keep using it, our brain gets used to it (called habituation), and it loses its effectiveness.

So, when you bring a talk, use novelty to create anticipation, but don't wait too long to give them your application, the take-away, or the benefit. Prime the curiosity pump.

Story

A very powerful way to pique interest in a talk comes through telling stories. Storytelling is as old as mankind, seen from paintings in caves thousands of years old to virtual reality today. Stories communicate deep truth, connect with our emotions, and make learning stick. Storytelling is an extremely effective way to communicate spiritual truth for life transformation.

In one interesting study[141] that illustrates the power of story to arrest attention, two writers collaborated on a project to discover the impact of adding meaning to otherwise meaningless objects. They bought $129 worth of knickknacks at thrift stores, with no item costing more than $2. They then recruited other writers to create stories related to these

---

[139] Simon, Kindle e-book loc. 1592.

[140] Michael I. Posner and Mary K. Rothbart, "Research on Attention Networks as a Model for the Integration of Psychological Science," *Annual Review of Psychology* 58 (2007): 1–23, https://doi.org/10.1146/annurev. psych.58.110405.085516.

[141] *Significant Objects | …and How They Got That Way*, accessed December 11, 2019, http://significantobjects.com/.

items and posted the items with their stories on eBay. What happened was amazing. Their experiment netted over $8,000. The stories created attention and impacted behavior.

The prototypical storyteller was Jesus Himself. The Gospels give many examples of His favorite teaching method—story—that we call parables. Parables communicate spiritual truths with earthly examples, and rabbis in Jesus' day often taught in parables. Mark records that, "He taught them many things by parables" (Mark 4:2). Those parables comprise a full quarter of His recorded words. And depending on how scholars count them, the total number of parables Jesus told range from the low 30s to over 60.[142] In a future chapter on emotion, I delve more deeply into story. But for now, remember that a good story is a powerful attention grabber.

Questions

Questions are another powerful tool in a communicator's toolbox. Over a century ago, education theorist Charles DeGarmo wrote, "In the skillful use of the question more than anything else lies the fine art of teaching: for in such use we have the guide to clear and vivid ideas, the quick spur to imagination, the stimulus to thought, the incentive to action."[143] And Jesus masterfully used questions with many— His disciples, individuals, small groups, and large crowds. I will deal with the power of questions in a future chapter as well, but a well-placed, provocative question can garner your listener's attention.

---

[142] *Teaching as Jesus Taught by Roy B. Zuck (9-Jan-2002) Paperback* (Wipf & Stock Publishers, 2002), p. 308.
[143] Charles de Garmo, *Interest and Education: The Doctrine of Interest and Its Concrete Application* (Palala Press, 2016) p. 179.

* * *

PRACTICE THREE: APPLY PRIMING

Priming is a way to nudge a listener in your direction. One philosopher coined the term *intuition pump* to refer to, "any metaphor or linguistic device that intuitively makes a conclusion seem more plausible."[144] The more familiar we are with something, the more we tend to accept it, even a falsehood. That's the power of priming. Nobel laureate Daniel Kahneman said, "A reliable way to make people believe in falsehoods is frequent repetition, because familiarity is not easily distinguished from truth."[145]

In one study, college students were asked to create sentences from sets of words. Half the words given to one student group related to elderly stereotypes like Florida, grey, and careful. The other half were given neutral words. After the task, the researchers secretly recorded how fast the students walked down a hallway. The ones who created sentences with words related to the elderly walked slower than the other students. This study illustrates what priming can do, even though it resulted in non-conscious behavior.[146] Advertisers use this technique often.

Here's an example of priming in a talk. In one of my sermons, I wanted to contrast what Scripture said about our material possessions with the common cultural perspective. So, I primed the congregation by explaining that I wanted

---

[144] Anderson, p. 89.

[145] Daniel Kahneman, *Thinking, Fast and Slow*, 1st edition (New York: Farrar, Straus and Giroux, 2013), p. 62.

[146] Bargh, J.A., Chen, M., & Burrows, L. (1996). Automaticity of social behavior: direct effects of trait construct and stereotype-activation on action. *Journal of personality and social psychology, 71 2*, 230-4.

them to contrast the difference between some Scriptures I immediately put on-screen and a short cartoon I showed of a prehistoric squirrel who represented a different perspective from Scripture (materialism). This exercise primed them (nudged them in my direction) to pay more attention to what followed.

* * *

So, in summary, *Principle Two: Attention ... Pique Interest* means we must intentionally build into our talks ways to create interest and capture our listener's attention so they will listen. I suggested three ways to do so. First, adapt your talk to the dynamics of attention. Second, add appropriate attention grabbers that include the neural cousins of novelty and curiosity, story, and questions, the latter two of which I will unpack in a future chapter. Finally, apply the concept of priming.

Principle Two: ATTENTION—PIQUE INTEREST

How can you get your listeners to listen?

o   Adapt your talk to the dynamics of attention.
o   Add appropriate attention grabbers.
o   Apply priming.

In the next chapter, we'll look at *Principle Three: Affinity ... Create Connection.*

* * *

APPLICATION

1. Practice a bit of a learning technique called "free recall" by taking three minutes to write down everything you can recall from reading about attention.
2. Look at the talk you evaluated in the prior chapter. How did you use the concept of attention? How could you have used it more effectively?
3. Think about curiosity and novelty and try to recall a talk you saw or heard where the speaker used novelty and curiosity. What did they do/say? Why did their use of curiosity and novelty affect your ability to recall the talk?

Check out the website for downloadable tools at
www.charlesstone.com/TEDfreebies

6

Principle Three: Affinity ...
Create Connection

Nobody cares how much you know until they know how much you care. —Teddy Roosevelt

---

Chapter Big Idea: Principle Three—*Affinity ... Create Connection* answers the question, *Why should your audience listen?*, the "So what?" question. Three key practices will help you apply this principle:

1. Know your material.
2. Know your audience.
3. Help the audience know (and like) you.

I earned my undergraduate degree in industrial engineering from GA Tech. I paid my way through school through a program that allowed me to work alternating quarters with an engineering firm. Occasionally, I'd take a night course during a work quarter.

I took one course three times—"dynamics," notorious for its difficulty. The first two times, I dropped the course because I felt totally lost. I could not understand what the professors was trying to teach, and those first two profs felt as cold as a freezer to us students. The third time I took the course, however, I made an A.

What made the difference?

The professor did.

This professor conveyed genuine warmth to each student. He willingly answered our questions. He would meet with us after class. Although he knew his material quite well, he also knew that most students struggled with this course. So, he brought it down to our level rather than teaching it at his high level.

I don't know if he had studied communication and the brain, but because he understood those principles, he created an affinity with us which helped us learn better.

In this chapter, we'll look at how you can develop affinity with your listeners by connecting with them through three practices.

* * *

PRACTICE ONE: KNOW YOUR MATERIAL

One important way you can create affinity with your audience is by knowing what you're talking about. People listen to communicators who clearly know their material. It brings them authority.

Although Jesus did not graduate from one of the rabbinical schools, He showed a profound, intuitive knowledge of the Old Testament Scriptures. John writes this about Jesus when he spoke at a Jewish feast, "Not until halfway through the feast did Jesus go up to the temple courts and begin to teach. The Jews were amazed and asked, 'How did this man get such learning without having studied?'" (John 7:14-15) The people were amazed at His grasp of Scripture even though He lacked formal training.

Luke records an episode earlier in Jesus' life when He accompanied Mary and Joseph on one of the annual visits to Jerusalem to observe Passover. At this time, Jesus was 12 years old. After the festival was over, unbeknownst to His parents, Jesus stayed back. After three days, they realized He was not with the caravan, so they went back to Jerusalem and found Him in the temple courts. Luke writes that when they found Him, He was "sitting among the teachers, listening to them and asking them questions. Everyone who heard him was amazed at his understanding and his answers" (Luke 2:46-47). Almost 20 years before He began His public ministry, He already had a stunning understanding of the Scriptures.

As Professor Roy Zuck writes, Jesus "displayed full mastery of what He taught. He was never dependent on notes, never at a loss for what to say, never unprepared, never taken aback or confused by a question from friend or foe, never unsure of what to communicate."[147]

Jesus spoke with authority, and the people noticed. Matthew wrote that, "He taught as one who had authority, and not as their teachers of the law" (Matt. 7:29). Of course, Jesus had intrinsic authority as the Son of God. Although we don't have that kind of authority, command of our subject matter will give us derived authority in our learners' minds.

Your knowledge of your material will help your learners create an emotional connection to it. That is, the authority

---

[147] *Teaching as Jesus Taught by Roy B. Zuck (9-Jan-2002) Paperback* (Wipf & Stock Publishers, 2002), p. 54.

you bring can help them see the value of it from both a cognitive and an emotional perspective (related to salience). And if your listeners lack such emotional connection, it can hinder learning. Neuroscientist Mary Helen Immordino-Yang notes, "Factual knowledge alone is useless without a guiding emotional intuition […] if they feel no connection to the knowledge they learn […], [the] content will seem emotionally meaningless to them."[148] Such connection will help create ownership of their learning because they see and emotionally experience the value of it. The more positive emotion you evoke toward the material in your talk, the more your listeners will be engaged and will learn.[149]

* * *

PRACTICE TWO: KNOW YOUR AUDIENCE

The curator of the popular TED talks makes a strong case to know your audience, "Language works its magic only to the extent that it is shared by speaker and listener. And there's the key clue to how to achieve the miracle of re-creating your idea in someone else's brain. You can only use the tools that your audience has access to. If you start only with your language, your concepts, your assumptions, your values, you will fail. So instead, start with theirs. It's only from that common ground that they can begin to build your idea inside their minds."[150]

---

[148] Mary Helen Immordino-Yang, Antonio Damasio, and Howard Gardner, *Emotions, Learning, and the Brain: Exploring the Educational Implications of Affective Neuroscience*, 1 edition (New York: W. W. Norton & Company, 2015), p. 104.

[149] Barbara L. Fredrickson, "The Role of Positive Emotions in Positive Psychology," *The American Psychologist* 56, no. 3 (March 2001): 218–26.

[150] Anderson, Kindle e-book loc. 343.

In other words, imagine you are in the audience, and let that drive what you plan to say.

The better you know your audience, the better you'll be able to adapt and match your message to their needs, desires, backgrounds, and the fact that people learn at different rates.[151] We certainly can't read minds, and we don't know what people are thinking or their heart condition, as Jesus did (John 2:23-25). He perfectly understood hearts, what people were thinking, and their motivations. He understood His enemies (Matt. 12:25), His friends, and His inquirers. Although we don't have that ability, we must still try to understand our audience the best we can.

Jesus matched His teaching to His audience and created an affinity to Himself, though not always. The religious elite felt threatened and had Him crucified, but in general, crowds and individuals were drawn to Him. He knew their hearts and adapted His teaching to His audience. He even withheld some teaching because His listeners could not fully bear what He had to say (John 16:12).

To one inquisitive student, Nicodemus, He used give-and-take communication and evocative language to make that ruler consider deep truths about salvation (John 3:1-21). To a Samaritan woman involved in sexual sin, He used the image of clean, pure water to create a spiritual thirst in her for Living Water, Himself (John 4:1-42). In response to the Pharisees who thought Jesus was guilty of blasphemy after seeing Him heal a paralyzed man and forgive his sins, He directly addressed their thoughts, "Knowing their thoughts, Jesus said, 'Why do you entertain evil thoughts in your hearts?' Which is easier: to say, 'Your sins are forgiven,' or to say, 'Get up and walk'?

---

[151] Harvey Whitehouse, "Modes of Religiosity," *The Council of Societies for the Study of Religion Bulletin* 37, no. 4 (November 2008): 108–12.

But so that you may know that the Son of Man has authority on earth to forgive sins. Then he said to the paralytic, 'Get up, take your mat and go home.' And the man got up and went home" (Matt. 9:4-7). Jesus knew His audience and matched His teaching to it.

Lev Vygotsky, an early educational theorist, is known for a concept called the zone of proximal development—the distance between what a learner can do on their own and what they need help with. Communicators can guide learners to the next level of understanding by providing scaffolding or help (guidance, feedback, resources, etc.) so they can understand what they need to know to get to the next level and stay there. It's building upon prior knowledge.

Experts Versus Novices

In every audience, whether a classroom, a worship gathering, or a business setting, not everyone is equally versed in the subject you're teaching. The learners represent a wide range of prior knowledge of the subject matter. Some who know a lot about it might be called experts. On the other end of the spectrum would lie the novices—those who know little. Every setting includes people along this spectrum.

The range of your listeners poses a challenge for most communicators. For example, let's say a math teacher is given a class of 30 students and is tasked to generically teach them math. Those 30 students range from 1st grade to 12th grade, all with varying math skills. What's a teacher to do? Teach addition, division, multiplication, calculus, or what? To whom does that teacher direct the lesson?

That is akin to many learning environments and poses a particular challenge to pastors who bring a message each Sunday. Some of the attendees have no theological background (pure novices), while some have been in the faith for decades and have extensive theological knowledge (experts). How does a pastor tailor a talk to connect to and facilitate learning for such a wide variety of learners, from pure novices to expert experts? Your audience may not reflect this large of a gap, but you must still acknowledge the disparity and plan your talks with this in mind.

Degrees in prior knowledge make a profound difference in how learners learn and think. Although an expert and a novice may have similar IQs and working-memory capacity, they will approach learning differently.

Experts can process more information than novices because they can process domain-specific information quickly through something called chunking (a way to put more information into smaller packages, more about that in the next chapter). They have understanding of deep structures and principles about the material, whereas a novice first focuses on surface issues. This deep understanding gives experts a form of intuition that novices lack. They can more quickly make connections and draw conclusions. While a novice might lose interest if the information is too complex, an expert will feel motivated to persist and rise to the learning challenge. And the more someone knows, the greater their capacity to deeply understand.

Psychologist Robert Glaser noted six characteristics that set experts apart from novices:[152]

1. Their competence relates to a specific area of expertise.
2. They notice patterns and what's important more easily than novices.

---

[152] Robert Glaser, *The Nature of Expertise*, National Center for Research in Vocational Education (National Center Publications, 1985).

3. Their ability in pattern recognition enables them to quickly use their knowledge and encode larger chunks of information. This means experts experience less cognitive load than a novice (cognitive load means strain on working memory, more on that in a later chapter).

4. They see relationships within elements of those patterns because they make connections to the larger goals.

5. They more skillfully use attention because they aren't using up their cognitive bandwidth. They can mentally pause and step back to see the big picture and can quickly find solutions. This may slow them down at the beginning as they observe the processes necessary for solving the problem, but in the end, their ability to self-regulate results in faster problem solving.

6. They can adapt their expertise easily.

So how might understanding the differences between novices and experts in your audience affect how you communicate?[153] First, simply recognize the wide range of learners in your audience. Second, if your audience is on-going, provide repeated exposure to the content. By doing so, you'll create more automaticity in the novices' thinking which will leave more working memory available to process new information you bring. Third, build brief pauses into your talks when you ask your learners to step back and think about what they are thinking about with respect to what you just covered. It's called metacognition. Fourth, keep the big ideas before them. Fifth, if your setting allows for it, build time into your presentation to encourage conversations about the material among

---

[153] Diane Halpern, *Enhancing Thinking Skills in the Sciences and Mathematics*, (Routledge), 1992.

your learners. This is called social learning which can help novices learn from experts in the group.

I'll address visuals in a later chapter, but in this section on experts and novices, it's helpful to know that novices probably learn better from a picture with text about that picture. Experts, however, probably only need one source, a picture or text. This idea is called the expertise reversal effect. That is, what may help a novice learn (the picture with text) has the reverse effect on an expert.[154]

One other helpful insight, understanding the curse of knowledge, will help you become more like my professor in the opening story in this chapter. You'll recall he tailored his expert knowledge to us students who were novices on the subject.

Communication experts Chip and Dan Heath write about the curse of knowledge, "The problem is that once we know something—say, the melody of a song—we find it hard to imagine not knowing it. Our knowledge has 'cursed' us. We have difficulty sharing it with others, because we can't readily re-create their state of mind."[155] Our familiarity with material makes it difficult for us to feel what it means not to know it. Writing expert Steven Pinker notes that overcoming the curse of knowledge may be the single most important step to clear writing.[156] The same idea holds true for speaking. When you craft your talk, question the assumptions you are making

---

[154] Slava Kalyuga and Alexander Renkl, "Expertise Reversal Effect and Its Instructional Implications: Introduction to the Special Issue," *Instructional Science* 38, no. 3 (May 1, 2010): 209–15, https://doi.org/10.1007/s11251-009-9102-0.

[155] Chip Heath and Dan Heath, "The Curse of Knowledge," *Harvard Business Review*, December 1, 2006, https://hbr.org/2006/12/the-curse-of-knowledge.

[156] Steven Pinker, *The Sense of Style: The Thinking Person's Guide to Writing in the 21st Century*, Reprint edition (New York, New York: Penguin Books, 2015), chapter 3.

about your learners. You'll most likely discover that you've assumed your learners know more than they actually do.

Different Learning Capacities

It's easy for communicators to assume that everybody possesses the same learning capacities that they themselves do. They don't. In addition to prior knowledge, other factors affect learning. Stress, lack of sleep, poverty, working memory, processing speed, attentional ability, learning disabilities, and hearing ability all affect a person's ability to learn. Learning preferences (not learning styles as that has proven to be a myth), personality type, learning strategies, their beliefs about learning and thinking, and their motivation to learn also affect learning.[157] You may not know your audience very well, but you can assume that most people's ability to learn is compromised in some way. Keep that in mind as you develop and deliver your talk. One study found the more vivid you make your message through stories, picturesque examples, metaphors, quotes, and memorable imageries, the more you can enhance your talk's persuasiveness and memorability.[158]

It's also important to understand that we all *perceive* things differently. One learner in your audience may perceive your ideas differently from what the person sitting next to them may perceive. Cognitive psychologists Sumeracki and Weinstein make this helpful contrast between what we sense and what we perceive:

---

[157] Marilla D. Svinicki, "New Directions in Learning and Motivation," *New Directions for Teaching & Learning* 1999, no. 80 (Winter 1999): 5, https://doi.org/10.1002/tl.8001.

[158] Svinicki.

The difference between sensation and perception serves to explain why we don't always experience the world exactly how it is, or in the same way as the next person. When we talk about perception, we usually distinguish between bottom-up and top-down processing of information. Bottom-up processing begins and ends with the stimulus: you focus on the information coming from whatever you are trying to perceive, and you try to understand it just by using this information. Though we are always using bottom-up processing, we are usually also engaged in top-down processing, whereby we use our knowledge to understand something. This top-down processing can result in different interpretations of the information and strategies we try to teach our students, as well as a "curse of knowledge" that makes it difficult for us to see things through a novice's eyes.[159]

These concepts have powerful implications for spiritual formation, the transformation of the heart which leads to changes in attitude and action, character and conduct, and belief and behavior.[160]

How well you can know your audience depends on your setting. If you are a schoolteacher, you will spend hundreds of hours with students which give ample time to know them well. However, if you are giving a talk to a crowd once or you

---

[159] Yana Weinstein, Megan Sumeracki, and Oliver Caviglioli, *Understanding How We Learn: A Visual Guide*, 1 edition (London; New York, NY: Routledge, 2018), p. 48.

[160] Christopher B Beard, "Connecting Spiritual Formation and Adult Learning Theory: An Examination of Common Principles," *Christian Education Journal* 14, no. 2 (2017): 247–69.

are a guest preacher at a church, it will be more difficult to know your audience.

Personal Salience

Jesus knew His audience well, and He particularly knew what was important to them. Salience[161] is the term used to describe how something gets our attention, is noticeable or prominent, and it is based on how we rate its distinctiveness, perceived importance, value, or interest to us. Jesus picked illustrations and used everyday objects that mattered to His audience—farming metaphors for farmers, fishing illustrations for fishermen, building concepts for builders, etc. He used simple things of great importance to His listeners, such as water, bread, salt, wineskins, light, garments, etc.

The Increased Saliency Theory states, "Attentional resources constantly shift around so that some things become more salient than others—that is, more noticeable or important."[162] In other words, our brain constantly looks for something more interesting or prominent than what it's currently focused on at the moment. That's why it is so easy for your learners to get distracted. Salience has built into our brains a natural tendency to get distracted.

Saliency impacts your learners' personal motivation as well.[163] Your learners will listen to you better if they can connect your message to what's important to them. When they feel that what you are saying is relevant, important, or

---

[161] The parts of the brain that comprise the salience network include the insula, the amygdala, the anterior cingulate cortex, and the hypothalamus.

[162] Weinstein, Sumeracki, and Caviglioli, p. 54.

[163] Michael S. Fine and Brandon S. Minnery, "Visual Salience Affects Performance in a Working Memory Task," *Journal of Neuroscience* 29, no. 25 (June 24, 2009): 8016–21, https://doi.org/10.1523/JNEUROSCI.5503-08.2009.

related to a personal goal, their emotions get engaged which release hormones and neurotransmitters. As a result, connection to their salience enhances their alertness, memory, and learning.[164]

Yet, without the power of Christ, life can become all about me and my wants (*What's salient to me?*). Therein lies another challenge for Christian communicators. How can we help our learners shift attention, focus, and effort from a me-centric life (*What's in it for me?*) to a Christ-centric life (*What would most please Him?*)?

* * *

PRACTICE THREE: HELP THE AUDIENCE KNOW AND LIKE YOU

Earlier, I referred to Vygotsky's zone of proximal development. This concept was posthumously published in the book, *Mind in Society*. He defined this zone as, "the distance between the actual developmental level as determined by individual problem solving and the level of potential development as determined through problem solving under adult guidance or in collaboration with more capable peers."[165] He captured the role relationships play in learning. Learners need others to help them learn.

The relationship you build with your learners will profoundly impact their ability to learn. Even if you don't

---

[164] Sarah Rose Cavanagh, *The Spark of Learning: Energizing the College Classroom with the Science of Emotion*, 1st edition (Morgantown, West Virginia: West Virginia University Press, 2016), p. 44.

[165] L. S. Vygotsky, *Mind in Society: Development of Higher Psychological Processes*, ed. Michael Cole et al., Revised ed. edition (Harvard University Press, 1980), p. 84.

personally know your audience members, you can still create a connection with them to enhance their learning and receptivity to you. An authentic relationship with your learners will build trust that is much needed when real transformation through learning can be perceived as threatening and emotionally charged (because it means change and change is scary).[166]

One review of 1,400 student ratings of lessons revealed that a student's personal connection with the teacher, called social presence, was the number one factor that influenced learner satisfaction.[167] Five factors increase social presence:[168]

1. Social respect—a sense that the communicator acknowledges their contributions
2. Social sharing—interpersonal exchange between learner and communicator
3. Open mind—a sense where learners feel free to share their beliefs and values
4. Social identity—learners and communicators use personal names
5. Intimacy—freedom to share personal information

People were attracted to Jesus not only by what He taught but by who He was. He drew sinners, publicans, outcasts, children, and crowds to Himself because they enjoyed being with Him. They liked Him. And when the rich young ruler walked away from Jesus, "Jesus looked at him and loved him"

---

[166] Jack Mezirow and Edward W. Taylor, eds., *Transformative Learning in Practice: Insights from Community, Workplace, and Higher Education*, 1 edition (San Francisco, CA: Jossey-Bass, 2009), p. 13.
[167] Mayer, p. 863.
[168] Mayer, p. 863.

(Mark 10:21). Even though the man rejected Him, Jesus had a personal connection to him.

The method Jesus used to train His disciples and connect to them, perhaps difficult to do today, involved them literally following Him around. They learned about God through this relationship. Out of this teaching method rose the saying, "You should learn from a rabbi by 'covering yourself in his dust.'" That is, by following so closely with Jesus, the dust on His feet would cling to their clothes.[169]

As you encourage and convey support and caring, you "stimulate [your learners'] neural circuitry to learn, priming their brains for neuroplastic processes."[170] In fact, when people like you, feel safe around you, and feel that they belong, the brain releases oxytocin, a neurotransmitter popularly referred to as the brain's "trust" hormone. When that happens, our fear circuits and stress are dampened[171] which enhances learning.[172] Ultimately, your listener will learn best when they feel you care about them.[173] They may even view you as a better communicator. One study noted that subordinates who liked

---

[169] Lois Tverberg and Ray Vander Laan, *Walking in the Dust of Rabbi Jesus: How the Jewish Words of Jesus Can Change Your Life* (Grand Rapids, Mich.: Zondervan, 2013), p. 28.

[170] Louis Cozolino, *The Social Neuroscience of Education: Optimizing Attachment and Learning in the Classroom* (W. W. Norton & Company, 2013), p.17.

[171] Izelle Labuschagne et al., "Oxytocin Attenuates Amygdala Reactivity to Fear in Generalized Social Anxiety Disorder," *Neuropsychopharmacology: Official Publication of the American College of Neuropsychopharmacology* 35, no. 12 (November 2010): 2403–13, https://doi.org/10.1038/npp.2010.123.

[172] Sarah K. Fineberg and David A. Ross, "Oxytocin and the Social Brain," *Biological Psychiatry* 81, no. 3 (February 1, 2017): e19–21, https://doi.org/10.1016/j.biopsych.2016.11.004.

[173] Christi Bergin and David Bergin, "Attachment in the Classroom," *Educational Psychology Review* 21, no. 2 (June 1, 2009): 141–70, https://doi.org/10.1007/s10648-009-9104-0.

their boss rated them higher in authenticity, transformational leadership, and ethics.[174]

Jesus cared deeply about people. As a Shepherd, He cared for His sheep. He had compassion on others because they were "like sheep without a shepherd" (Matt. 9:36).

In fact, if a communicator balances encouragement with appropriate challenge, these neurotransmitters conducive for learning get activated—dopamine, serotonin, norepinephrine, and endorphins.[175]

You want to build trust with your learners. You hope to build a new idea in their minds which means they must open them to you. If your audience is brand new, you are essentially asking a stranger to open up to another stranger. In that case, you want to disarm their concerns early on. Simple things like good eye contact, a genuine smile, humor, and perhaps a bit of self-disclosure can help foster trust, similar to a western movie when the big burly guy walks into the saloon and opens his coat to show that he doesn't have a gun.

Vulnerability is powerful, but too much of it can backfire. Author Brene Brown writes this about vulnerability:

> Formulaic or contrived personal sharing leaves audiences feeling manipulated and often hostile toward you and your message. Vulnerability is not oversharing. There's a simple equation: vulnerability minus boundaries is not vulnerability. It can be anything from an attempt to hotwire connection to attention-seeking, but it's not vulnerability and it doesn't lead to connection. The best way I've found to get clear on this is

[174] "An Exploration of the Role of Subordinate Affect in Leader Evaluations. - PsycNET," accessed July 10, 2020, https://doi.apa.org/record/2018-12590-001?doi=1.
[175] Cozolino, p. 18.

to really examine our intentions. Is sharing done in service of the work on stage or is it a way to work through our own stuff? The former is powerful, the latter damages the confidence people have in us.[176]

Many people in your audiences come laden with chronic stress and broken relationships which can turn the brain off to learning. However, when you convey caring and support, you can create the environment that helps mitigate those negative consequences by priming the brain for "curiosity, exploration, and learning."[177]

Jesus profoundly connected to hurting people—from a prostitute to a hated tax collector to sick people to children. He was known as a friend of sinners. The common everyday people simply liked Jesus.

Humor

A happy learner is a good learner. When people laugh with you, they tend to like you more. And when they like you more, they learn better. Significant amounts of research indicate that positive emotions, like happiness, help people learn. One way to foster this is to convey your happiness and joy with your subject matter. Emotional contagion, our ability to "catch" another's emotions, helps create a happy learning environment (more on emotional contagion later).

When you use humor, learners focus their attention because humor brings the unexpected and drives learning deeper. Professor Sarah Cavanagh writes, "In the presence of humor, students detect and then have to resolve the incongruity

---

[176] Anderson, p. 52.
[177] Cozolino, p. 49.

between their original expectations and the humorous twist. This process of making one interpretation and then having to revise it results in a deeper level of mental processing than being exposed to the correct interpretation from the beginning; one is required to relate the information to more than one set of concepts and ideas, to reflect and elaborate on both the meaning of the initial interpretation and the revised interpretation."[178] In other words, humor violates our expectations in a harmless way which requires the learner to process information in a deeper way, thus enhancing learning.

Humor also helps reduce anxiety which improves learning.[179] It activates many brain regions, especially those related to relational attachment and those involved in resolving novel information. It stimulates brain growth, increases attention[180] and retention, and enhances memory.[181] [182] It also fuels the brain because when we laugh, we get more oxygen into our bloodstreams, and the brain needs oxygen to function well. It can cause an endorphin surge. Endorphins, the body's natural pain killer, makes us feel good. "Laughing during learning seems to increase curiosity and enhance subsequent memory,"[183] thus enhancing learning.

---

[178] Cavanagh, p. 75.

[179] Ronald Berk, "Does Humor in Course Tests Reduce Anxiety and Improve Performance?," *College Teaching* 48 (October 1, 2000): 151–58, https://doi.org/10.1080/87567550009595834.

[180] Sousa, p. 73.

[181] Cozolino, p. 88-91.

[182] Daniela Jeder, "Implications of Using Humor in the Classroom," *Procedia - Social and Behavioral Sciences*, The 6th International Conference Edu World 2014 "Education Facing Contemporary World Issues", 7th - 9th November 2014, 180 (May 5, 2015): 828–33, https://doi.org/10.1016/j.sbspro.2015.02.218.

[183] Rana Esseily et al., "Humour Production May Enhance Observational Learning of a New Tool-Use Action in 18-Month-Old Infants," *Cognition and Emotion* 30, no. 4 (May 18, 2016): 817–25, https://doi.org/10.1080/02699931.2015.1036840.

Professor Roy Zuck writes, "As the world's greatest Communicator-Teacher, Jesus frequently employed humor to great advantage."[184] But it was always purposeful and never cruel, sarcastic, or bitter. Illustrations Jesus used, such as a Pharisee blowing a trumpet to announce his offering (Matt. 6:2), the image of a large plank sticking out of a judgmental person's eye (Matt. 7:3), or the visual of a camel crawling through the eye of a needle (Matt. 19:24), must have brought chuckles to His learners. In fact, theologian Elton Trueblood, who decades ago served as a chaplain at Harvard and Stanford, even wrote a book entitled, *The Humor of Christ*.

A simple smile can help you connect to your audience. Smiling makes us feel better, makes us look more attractive and competent, and stimulates our brains better than chocolate. A smile is also contagious.[185] So genuine smiling during a talk can help endear you to those you hope to influence. When matched with a conversational tone, a smile and humor will make your listener want to listen and learn even more.[186]

Although the Gospels don't explicitly say that Jesus smiled, for several reasons, I believe He often did so. He was human and experienced the full range of human emotions. He was full of the joy of the Holy Spirit, and joy makes you smile. Children clamored to be with Him, and kids are drawn to kind people who smile. He was criticized because lost people wanted to be with Him. Hurting and broken people aren't drawn to negative, dour people. Author John Eldridge even

[184] Zuck, p. 204.

[185] Daniela Jeder, "Implications of Using Humor in the Classroom," *Procedia - Social and Behavioral Sciences*, The 6th International Conference Edu World 2014 "Education Facing Contemporary World Issues", 7th - 9th November 2014, 180 (May 5, 2015): 828–33, https://doi.org/10.1016/j.sbspro.2015.02.218.

[186] Mayer, *The Cambridge Handbook of Multimedia Learning*, p. 346.

devotes an entire chapter in his book, *Beautiful Outlaw*,[187] to Jesus' playfulness.

* * *

So, in summary, *Principle Three: Affinity ... Create Connection* means that we seek to connect to our learners. I suggested three ways to do so. First, know your material. Second, know your audience. Third, help your audience know (and like) you.

Principle Three: AFFINITY—CREATE CONNECTION

Why should your audience listen, the "So what?" question.

o   Know your material.
o   Know your audience.
o   Help the audience know (and like) you.

In the next chapter, we'll look at *Principle Four: Capacity ... Free Up Working Memory*.

* * *

---

[187] John Eldredge, *Beautiful Outlaw: Experiencing the Playful, Disruptive, Extravagant Personality of Jesus*, Reprint edition (New York: FaithWords, 2013).

APPLICATION

1. In your unique setting, what could you do to know your audience better?
2. What do you think is salient to them?
3. How might you shift your learners from a focus on personal salience to more of a focus on what's important to God?
4. How might you build a deeper relationship with your learners?

Check out the website for downloadable tools at
www.charlesstone.com/TEDfreebies

7

Principle Four: Capacity ...
Free up Working Memory

Everything in life is memory, save for the thin edge of the present. *—Michael Gazzaniga*[188]

Chapter Big Idea: Principle Four—*Capacity ... Free Up Working Memory* answers the question, *How can you beat the competition vying for the same brain space of your learners?* Three key practices will help you apply this principle:

1. Maximize all the components of working memory.
2. Minimize cognitive load.
3. Marry new knowledge to prior knowledge.

---

[188] Michael Gazzaniga, quoted in Endel Tulving and Fergus Craik (eds), *The Oxford Handbook of Memory* (New York: Oxford University Press, 2005), p. 703.

I wrote this chapter about three months after the COVID-19 pandemic hit North America. My wife and I had just returned from vacation on a Thursday, and the next day, we drove from Toronto to London, Ontario, where we lived. That Friday afternoon, the Canadian government shut everything down, including churches. As lead pastor of our church, I called an emergency staff meeting to set in motion our plans to deliver ministry online for the unforeseeable future.

The pandemic radically changed life for everyone. I'm resilient and goal oriented, so I quickly switched into my leadership mode and helped the church navigate through this unprecedented change. I initially worked 25 straight days with only one day off (not my regular practice, but necessary in a crisis).

I settled into a routine after the initial adrenaline rush, and I began to realize that I couldn't concentrate as well as I once did. My mind wandered more easily. I couldn't seem to focus when I sat down at my computer to write a sermon or send an email. I forget things more easily. I couldn't learn or remember as quickly as I once did. Our church staff began to share with me that they also faced similar symptoms, and I read many online posts that other pastors experienced the same. Was this a symptom of COVID-19? Did I have it?

No, I didn't have COVID-19.

I, my team, and almost everybody else I knew experienced similar cognitive challenges, including decreased focus, increased mind wandering, and more forgetfulness. As I dug deeper, I learned about a brain basis behind these symptoms related to working memory. The generalized anxiety we all felt had temporarily compromised working memory. And when working memory gets compromised for whatever reason, our ability to learn also gets compromised.[189]

Your learners' working memory, COVID-19 or not, profoundly affects their ability to learn from your talks. Yet, by applying the working memory insights that follow, you'll be able to bolster your learners' working memory and provide a boost that will help them learn better because durable learning doesn't happen without an engaged working memory. In this chapter, you'll learn three ways to increase your learners' learning capacities by freeing up working memory and making it work more efficiently.

* * *

PRACTICE ONE: MAXIMIZE ALL THE COMPONENTS OF WORKING MEMORY

You'll recall from Chapter 3 that we have three kinds of memory—sensory memory (which lasts a few seconds), working memory (which lasts 30 seconds or so), and long-term memory (which lasts much longer).

I explained that working memory holds new information, reaches back to long-term memory to retrieve related information, combines that existing knowledge with the new information, and then sends it back to long-term memory for storage and later retrieval. It's like a bridge between what we perceive and our future actions.[190]

---

[189] Tim P. Moran, "Anxiety and Working Memory Capacity: A Meta-Analysis and Narrative Review," *Psychological Bulletin* 142, no. 8 (2016): 831–64, https://doi.org/10.1037/bul0000051.

[190] Adam Gazzaley and Larry D. Rosen, *The Distracted Mind: Ancient Brains in a High-Tech World*, Reprint edition (The MIT Press, 2016), p. 34.

The efficiency of working memory depends on these four factors:[191]

- *The Who*—the knowledge, processing skills, and abilities of the learner
- *The What*—the type of information the learner must remember and the degree the information is familiar
- *The How*—the processing demands of the learning task (i.e., how much attention is necessary and what distractions must be inhibited)
- *The Where*—the characteristics of the learning environment

Working memory includes four components, based on the working memory model by Baddeley and Hitch.[192] In Chapter 3, I summarized this model, and I've added a bit more explanation below as a refresher, including the diagram again:

- The *conductor or CEO (called the central executive)*—The conductor drives the entire process in the following ways: it allocates incoming data to the other parts of working memory, it monitors and coordinates the inner eye and the inner voice/ear, and it drives attention.
- The *inner eye (called the visio-spatial sketchpad)*—It stores and rehearses visual information. It stores the where and what and has a limited capacity.[193]

[191] Singer and Bashir, "Wait. . . What?"

[192] Baddeley, Eysenck, and Anderson, *Memory*.

[193] Richard E. Mayer and Roxana Moreno, "Nine Ways to Reduce Cognitive Load in Multimedia Learning," *Educational Psychologist* 38, no. 1 (March 2003): 43–52, https://doi.org/10.1207/S15326985EP3801_6.

- The *inner ear/inner voice (called the phonological loop)*—It processes, stores, and rehearses speech. The inner ear perceives speech, and the inner voice is involved in producing speech, both vocalized and sub-vocalized. It has a limited capacity.
- The *mixer or backup storage (called the episodic buffer)*—This serves as the working memory's storage component and receives information from the conductor (which has received information from the inner eye and the inner ear/voice), from information coming from our five senses, and from long-term memory. While maintaining a sense of time and keeping things in sequence, it manipulates and binds (mixes) all the information together into chunks as a unified whole and sends that chunked information to long-term memory for consolidation (the process by which memories "stick"). It is limited to four chunks of material, four +/- two.[194] We might also describe this part of working memory similar to a computer's RAM with long-term memory like a computer's ROM.

---

[194] Nelson Cowan, "The Magical Mystery Four: How Is Working Memory Capacity Limited, and Why?," *Current Directions in Psychological Science* 19, no. 1 (February 1, 2010): 51–57, https://doi.org/10.1177/0963721409359277.

WORKING MEMORY
5 SENSES

SIGHT HEARING TOUCH SMELL TASTE

VISUAL (INNER EYE)
(VISIO-SPATIAL
SKETCHPAD)

VERBAL (INNER EAR/
VOICE)
(PHONOLOGICAL
LOOP)

(CENTRAL
EXECUTIVE)

(EPISODIC
BUFFER)

(LONG-TERM MEMORY)

Most talks will combine both the visual and the verbal parts of working memory. This relates to the concept called *dual coding*.[195] That is, when we combine the visual (inner eye) with the verbal (inner ear/inner voice) as both channels work somewhat simultaneously, working memory gets maximized and learning deepens because information has been processed

---

[195] James M. Clark and Allan Paivio, "Dual Coding Theory and Education," *Educational Psychology Review* 3, no. 3 (1991): 149–210, https://doi.org/10.1007/BF01320076.

through two different channels. This is like how a two-lane road allows more traffic than a one-lane road. We simply learn things more deeply from words *and* pictures than we do from words alone.[196] With two routes to retrieval, if one is lost, the other one may survive to allow recall.[197] It's called the multi-media principle or modality effect. And, "A picture is memorable when it is easy to label, and text is memorable when it is easy to picture."[198]

In one study to determine how to help elementary students remember and follow oral instructions, the group that received both verbal and visual instruction remembered the instructions better after several months.[199] In another study, researchers asked participants to try to remember up to 10,000 pictures presented once every five seconds. Incredibly, they remembered more that 70% of them in a later forced-choice recognition test.[200]

Our brain processes pictures more quickly and easily in working memory than it processes words. It's called the picture superiority effect.[201] A picture really is worth a thousand (or more) words. Visual tools help language stand still.[202]

---

[196] Mayer, p. 23.

[197] Baddeley, Eysenck, and Anderson, *Memory,* p. 170.

[198] Simon, Kindle e-book loc. 2448.

[199] Cynthia B. Gill et al., "Following Directions: Rehearsal and Visualization Strategies for Children with Specific Language Impairment," *Child Language Teaching and Therapy* 19, no. 1 (2003): 85–101, https://doi.org/10.1191/0265659003ct245oa.

[200] Lionel Standing, "Learning 10000 Pictures," *Quarterly Journal of Experimental Psychology* 25, no. 2 (May 1, 1973): 207–22, https://doi.org/10.1080/14640747308400340.

[201] Margaret Anne Defeyter, Riccardo Russo, and Pamela Louise McPartlin, "The Picture Superiority Effect in Recognition Memory: A Developmental Study Using the Response Signal Procedure," *Cognitive Development* 24, no. 3 (July 1, 2009): 265–73, https://doi.org/10.1016/j.cogdev.2009.05.002.

[202] Singer and Bashir, "Wait . . . What?"

Perhaps that's true because visual processing uses over 50% of our brain.[203]

When our brain stores visual images, it frees up working memory to better process verbal information. In essence, visual tools help our learners "hold" the language externally. They functionally expand working memory by creating external spaces where information is held. It would be like putting our salad (the visual image) in an external bowl so we have room to put our steak and potato on the limited space of our main plate. Without the salad bowl, the main plate would be crowded. And the more vivid the visual, the better we remember it (probably like the food visual I just gave you) because vividness arouses our emotions.[204] Our learners can manipulate new information on that main plate, while the external visual "bowl" holds the main concepts.

I wrote earlier that we can visualize working memory as a small chalkboard with limited space (four items, +/- one, in working memory). This size limitation often becomes a cognitive bottleneck that limits durable learning. Sometimes, we communicators inadvertently overload our listeners' working memory which limits durable learning. Although we can't technically increase the capacity of a learner's working memory, we can functionally improve it with techniques that free up what's there, thus avoiding the bottleneck so they can best learn.

Jesus masterfully blended the visual and the verbal for His learners. He often used object lessons by referring to or pointing out common, everyday items that people immediately knew, such as light, eyes, grain, flowers, birds, bread,

---

[203] Adam Fenster, "The Mind's Eye," *Rochester Review*, 2012, 6.

[204] Rebecca M. Todd et al., "Neurogenetic Variations in Norepinephrine Availability Enhance Perceptual Vividness," *Journal of Neuroscience* 35, no. 16 (April 22, 2015): 6506–16, https://doi.org/10.1523/JNEUROSCI.4489-14.2015.

gates, fruit, wolves, a yoke, fishing, doctors, crosses, a plow, vines, etc. When He made reference to them, He engaged His listeners' visual working memory. He then engaged their verbal working memory when He explained how that item related to the spiritual. As Warren Wiersbe wrote, "He turned His listeners' ears into eyes so they could see the truth and respond to it."[205]

Jesus not only used object lessons as visual teaching tools, but He also performed many miracles to reinforce His teaching. They became the ultimate object lessons. He instructed people with them as they pointed to His divine mission. They also showed His compassionate heart to relieve their suffering. The miracles made people take notice. After all, it would be hard to ignore a blind person who could now see or a lame person who could now walk.

Jesus also maximized working memory through visual metaphors. In a conversation with Nicodemus, He talked about being born again (John 3:1-21). He told His disciples that the temple would be raised in three days, referring to His resurrection (John 2:18-22), and He pointed to the urgency of evangelism when He pointed to grain fields ready for harvest (John 4:35). Martin Luther noted, "The common people were captivated more readily by [Jesus'] comparisons and examples than by difficult and subtle disputations. They would rather see a well-drawn picture than a well-written book."[206]

One reason metaphors and analogies enhance learning and memory lies in how the visual cortex processes images. It doesn't distinguish between what's imagined and what's real. When a learner imagines something in their mind's eye

---

[205] Warren W. Wiersbe, *Preaching and Teaching with Imagination: The Quest for Biblical Ministry*, Reprint edition (Grand Rapids: Baker Books, 1997), p. 160.
[206] Bennett, "Seasoned with Salt."

(because you effectively explain a visual in a talk), the same brain areas get activated as if they actually saw the thing or event (you actually use the visual in a talk).[207] Visual trumps verbal as does the vivid over the ordinary. A helpful equation that combines the visual with prior knowledge (see more on prior knowledge below) is this. Visual + vivid + prior knowledge helps create new knowledge. Educational experts have learned that using the arts can even enhance vividness to improve durable learning.

Jesus was *the* master of using visuals. He used images as wide ranging as coins and birds, splinters and stones, pigs and fish, and fire and figs. He used His most well-known visuals, wine and bread, in His last supper with the disciples. He used many visual images in His "I am" sayings describing Himself as bread, light, a door, the shepherd, and a vine. "He turned His listeners' ears into eyes so they could see the truth and respond to it,"[208] as noted above.

Comenius, a philosopher and pastor in the 17th century and considered to be the father of modern education, emphasized the visual when he wrote about the importance of adding pictures to texts.[209] Keep in mind, however, that a visual just for visual's sake will not aid learning. You'll want to make sure your learners remember not just the visual but also the concept you want the visual to demonstrate.[210] It may be difficult for learners with less knowledge of the subject to make the connection, so make sure you clearly explain the connection.

---

[207] Carmine Gallo, *Talk Like Ted*, Reprint edition (New York, USA: Smp Trade Paper, 2015), Kindle e-book loc. 3340.

[208] Wiersbe, p. 160.

[209] Mayer, p. 72.

[210] Kira J. Carbonneau, Scott C. Marley, and James P. Selig, "A Meta-Analysis of the Efficacy of Teaching Mathematics with Concrete Manipulatives," *Journal of Educational Psychology* 105, no. 2 (August 9, 2013): 380–400, https://doi.org/10.1037/a0031084.

We're all born with our unique working memory capacity. Technically, we can't grow working memory in our learners because genetics play such a significant role. And although some manufacturers of computerized brain games claim their games can expand working memory and make you smarter, at this point, supportive research is somewhat limited.[211] Playing such games may make you better at playing those particular games, but the skills probably won't transfer over into areas not related to that game, like general problem solving. Some people are simply born with greater working memory than others. Although you can't expand your learners' working memory, you can help it work most effectively with how you write and deliver your talks.

* * *

PRACTICE TWO: MINIMIZE COGNITIVE LOAD

As I've mentioned before, working memory can only handle so much information at once. Sometimes, we can inadvertently overload our listeners' working memory by giving too much material, going too fast, presenting in a complicated way, or assuming the learners know more than they actually do.

One theory related to this limited capacity is called *cognitive load theory* (CLT). This idea can help you avoid inadvertent mental overload. Since learning can't bypass working memory on its way to long-term memory, CLT[212] sheds light on what you can do to avoid a working memory bottleneck.

---

[211] Singer and Bashir, "Wait . . . What?"

[212] John Sweller, "Cognitive Load during Problem Solving: Effects on Learning," *Cognitive Science* 12, no. 2 (April 1, 1988): 257–85, https://doi.org/10.1016/0364-0213(88)90023-7.

CLT makes three fundamental assumptions that I've touched on earlier:[213]

1. People process information through two channels, one visual and one verbal.
2. Each of those channels has limited capacity to process information.
3. Learning occurs when people actively attend to the information. They do this by selecting what verbal and visual information they pay attention to, organizing both into a coherent mental framework, and then integrating the verbal and visual information into what they already know.

CLT also proposes that limited working memory is spread among three sources or processes that tax it. Don't let the titles below overload your working memory. Just try to understand the gist of what they mean.

Extraneous processing load—the mental effort the brain must dedicate to process *how* a topic is presented. It relates to the structure and manner you present the information to your learners. As a communicator, you influence this factor in the way you deliver subject material. You can make it hard or easy to learn, depending on *how* you present the material. For example, you could use a PowerPoint slide that includes a complex picture and multiple words which would tax working memory and unnecessarily increase extraneous load. This in turn would hinder learning. Or, you could use one with a simple picture and few words which results in low extraneous load and less strain on working memory.

---

[213] Mayer, p. 54.

Intrinsic or essential processing load—the mental effort the brain must dedicate to a specific learning topic, the mental effort dedicated to *learning the essentials of the material presented.* This relates to the inherent difficulty of a subject. For example, teaching how to solve 2+2 places less intrinsic load on a learner's brain than teaching how to solve a calculus problem. Essential load relates to the inherent difficulty of a subject. It is what we want our learner's working memory to be occupied with.

Germane or generative processing load—the mental effort the brain must dedicate to create long-term memories and *make sense* of the material presented. This is where the brain organizes and integrates material. This process involves constructing schemas, those neural manila folders I mentioned before, that hold information about specific topics.

Schemas free up working memory for other items because it treats a collection of information like it's one item. So, the more information in long-term memory in these schemas, the less load on short-term memory. They combine new learning with former learning by either assimilating the new information with what is known or accommodating it by creating new neural folders.[214]

When Jesus taught, He challenged existing beliefs (schemas). Whereas the Pharisees focused on external changes, Jesus focused on the heart which led to external changes. He "used the existing schema in the listener's mind as a starting point to propel the listener to establish new relationships and a new schema."[215]

---

[214] Terry Doyle, Todd D. Zakrajsek, and Kathleen F. Gabriel, *The New Science of Learning: How to Learn in Harmony With Your Brain*, 2 edition (Sterling, Virginia: Stylus Publishing, 2018), Kindle e-book loc. 1464.

[215] Lee, "Jesus Teaching Through Discovery."

All three of the processes above are additive. That is, if you add up the working memory required for each and the total exceeds the working memory capacity of your learner, you'll diminish how much learning occurs. So, a good communicator will design and deliver their teaching by keeping in mind these three processes that affect working memory.

What might be some practical ways CLT can help you create and deliver your presentations? I've organized some below around the three key processes noted above and called them communication goals.[216] Since working memory capacity is limited, we can get past that limitation somewhat through some of these techniques.

Communication Goal One—Minimize extraneous processing load. Don't complicate your talk.

- In your slides, remove unneeded material. Avoid fancy bells and whistles. Less is more.
- Highlight essential material with visual cues like arrows or different colors.
- Break up your talk into parts.
- When you use a graphic and text on a slide, place them close together. Better yet, show the picture first, and then the text.
- If you use extended text on a slide, let your learners read it to themselves first. Then you read it. Your learners read and comprehend at rates different from how you read and comprehend, so giving them time to read it

---

[216] For a detailed understanding of cognitive load theory and instructional goals in multimedia learning, see the *Cambridge Handbook of Multimedia Learning* by Richard E. Mayer, p. 61ff.

for themselves at their pace and skill will help reduce working memory load.

- When you talk about a graphic, put it on the screen at the same time you talk about it.

Communication Goal Two—Manage essential processing load.

- Use words and pictures instead of words alone.
- Use spoken text instead of printed text.
- Explain key elements of the subject that may be unfamiliar to your audience *before* you get into your talk or lesson (remember the concept map).
- Sequence the order you present your material from simplest to the more complex.

Communication Goal Three—Stimulate generative processing.

- Use a conversational tone.
- Have learners draw pictures of what they're learning.
- Give hints and feedback as learners solve problems or answer questions.
- Ask your learners to explain the subject to themselves or to another person.

Cognitive load theory provides a helpful framework, but two German scientists added another component[217] to make it even more helpful. To help reduce extraneous load (how you

---

[217] Thomas Huk and Stefan Ludwigs, "Combining Cognitive and Affective Support in Order to Promote Learning," *Learning and Instruction* 19, no. 6 (December 1, 2009): 495–505, https://doi.org/10.1016/j.learninstruc.2008.09.001.

present), they modified the idea by adding the emotional or affective component thus changing the acronym to "aCLT" for *augmented* cognitive load theory. This incorporates both the cognitive and the emotional component to maximize learning. It is "only when you boost their interest in the task that they [students/listeners] then dedicate these extra resources to learning and performance."[218] In Chapter 9, I detail how emotion can enhance learning.

Applying cognitive load insight can help your learners learn better. Minimize extraneous load (don't unnecessarily complicate your talk in how you deliver it), manage essential load (not too much, not too fast), and optimize generative load (motivate your learners to make connections to prior information in their neural manilla folders, their schemas).

In addition to the above suggestions, a concept called chunking can help reduce cognitive load. Chunking is a way to pack more information you want to remember into a smaller package more easily remembered. A word is an example of chunking. We don't consciously recall each letter when we read a word. Rather, we remember the word as a whole which is made up of the letters, so in effect, you remember the letters by recalling the word. And a piece of chunked information takes up about the same amount of space in memory as a single bit of information.

Mnemonics is a type of chunking. An example of mnemonics is the acronym HOMES which stands for names of the Great Lakes—Huron, Ontario, Michigan, Erie, and Superior. Another one we learned in school was *Please Excuse My Dear Aunt Sally* for the order to solve algebraic equations—parentheses, exponents, multiplication, division,

---

[218] Cavanagh, p. 39.

addition, and subtraction. Mnemonics work[219] because it gives us cues to jog our memory.

Jesus reduced cognitive load on His listeners' minds when He used well-known images and memorable statements like these. *Blessed are the pure in heart* (Matt. 5:8). *Ask and it shall be given to you* (Matt. 7:7). *Be perfect, therefore, as your heavenly Father is perfect* (Matt. 5:48). *No one can serve two masters* (Matt. 6:24). *For God so loved the world* (John 3:16). A writer from the prior century wrote, "Not from the musty tomes of rabbinical learning did Jesus extract antiquated incidents, but from the world in which people lived. He drew illustrations which all could understand and never forget."[220]

He often used what was common. When He taught spiritual lessons, He used objects common to the people, like bridesmaids, sheep, wineskins, and things in nature. This left open His hearers working memory and mental space so they could process and think about the new spiritual lesson He was teaching.

Every brain in every audience comes with information already filling their working memories. Their mental spotlights are already pointed at things other than the subject matter we want to present. Our task is to help them put into their working memories the information we want there. We want to help direct their spotlight of attention so they devote their working memory to the subject of our talk.

Reducing cognitive load will help your learners maximize their working memory. You don't want to overcomplicate

---

[219] Thomas Scruggs and Margo Mastropieri, "The Effectiveness of Mnemonic Instruction for Students with Learning and Behavior Problems: An Update and Research Synthesis," *Journal of Behavioral Education* 10 (September 1, 2000): 163–73, https://doi.org/10.1023/A:1016640214368.

[220] B H DeMent, "Principles and Methods of the Master Teacher," *Review & Expositor* 12, no. 1 (January 1915): 55–76.

your points to needlessly use up working memory, but you also don't want to make things so simple and familiar that you lull your listeners' brains to sleep.

* * *

PRACTICE THREE: MARRY NEW KNOWLEDGE
TO PRIOR KNOWLEDGE

A fundamental precept of learning is this—all new knowledge is based on prior knowledge. In one famous experiment, participants listened to this paragraph below and then the researchers tested their memory about the ideas in it:[221]

The procedure is actually quite simple. First you arrange things into different groups [...]. Of course, one pile may be sufficient depending on how much there is to do. If you have to go somewhere else due to lack of facilities that is the next step, otherwise you are pretty well set. It is important not to overdo any particular endeavor. That is, it is better to do too few things at once than too many. In the short run, this may not seem important, but complications from doing too many can easily arise. A mistake can be expensive as well [...]. At first the whole procedure will seem complicated. Soon, however, it will become just another facet of life. It is difficult to foresee any end to the necessity for this task in the immediate future, but then one never can tell. After the procedure is

---

[221] John D. Bransford and Marcia K. Johnson, "Contextual Prerequisites for Understanding: Some Investigations of Comprehension and Recall," *Journal of Verbal Learning and Verbal Behavior* 11, no. 6 (December 1, 1972): 717–26, https://doi.org/10.1016/S0022-5371(72)80006-9.

completed, one arranges the materials into different groups again. Then they can be put into their appropriate places. Eventually, they will be used once more and the whole cycle will have to be repeated. However, that is part of life.

This paragraph sounds weird if you don't know what it refers to, but if the paragraph began with the title, *Washing Clothes*, it makes sense. Once you know the subject, that prior knowledge makes the paragraph sensible. The participants in one group who were told beforehand it was about washing clothes remembered twice as much as those who were not told.

When you know relevant knowledge beforehand (i.e., this paragraph is about washing clothes), the brain builds upon related knowledge already in memory by connecting it to the new knowledge. It integrates both by making stronger connections, thus enhancing memory because these new associations help the brain retrieve new information when it's needed.

Prior knowledge is held in a mental model I've already explained as a schema, a "mental representation of what all instances of something have in common."[222] These neural folders help us remember, comprehend, and solve problems better, improve abstract thinking, and help us create relationships with disparate chunks of information.[223]

Unfortunately, some of the information in these neural manila folders is wrong. Communicators can't make these neural networks go away simply with a great talk, but we can apply these principles which, over time, can weaken those false networks as the Holy Spirit transforms the mind.

---

[222] James P. Byrnes, *Cognitive Development and Learning in Instructional Contexts*, 3 edition (Boston: Pearson, 2007), p. 26.
[223] Hardiman, Kindle e-book loc. 1848.

Prior knowledge acts like a filter to help the brain establish relevance and meaning and tap into existing neuronal pathways. Jesus modeled using prior knowledge. He often bridged what His learners knew with what He wanted them to learn and understand. He tailored His communication to the learner. In John 3:5, we see this when He speaks intellectually to the intellectual Nicodemus and speaks very personally to the Samaritan woman at the well about her need for living water. In Luke 24:13-35, before He reveals Himself to the men on the way to Emmaus, He leads them through a review about what they already knew of the prophets and prophecies.[224] Later, the men finally made the connection Jesus wanted them to make.

Jesus often married new knowledge to prior knowledge. He often said, *"You have heard it said* (prior knowledge), *but I tell you* (new knowledge)." When He used the parable of the sower (Matt. 13:3-9), He described four kinds of environments that seeds could be planted in. In an agrarian society, the farmers in Palestine would immediately have understood the four kinds of soils and the need for rich soil to produce a healthy crop. It would have been an easy mental jump for them to connect this to the condition of the heart to produce spiritual fruit. A leading learning theory, constructivism, states that learners learn when they build upon prior knowledge, synthesizing it into new knowledge.[225] Jesus helped His disciples, "construct their own experience based on what they had been taught."[226]

---

[224] Andrea Luxton, "The Bible and Pedagogy," *Faculty Publications*, March 15, 2004, https://digitalcommons.andrews.edu/english-pubs/21.

[225] John Holloway, "Caution: Constructivism Ahead - Educational Leadership," *Educational Leadership* 57, no. 3 (11/99): 85–86.

[226] Francine Anuarite K Wasukundi, "Pedagogy of Jesus for Modern World Christian Teachers," *AFER* 54, no. 3–4 (September 2012): 262–84.

* * *

So, in summary, *Principle Four: Capacity ... Free Up Working Memory* means that we should use techniques that help our learners use their working memory most efficiently. I suggested three ways to do this. First, understand working memory well enough to maximize the key components of it. Second, minimize cognitive load. Third, help your learners connect their prior knowledge of your talk's theme to the new information you're giving them.

Principle Four: *Capacity ... Free Up Working Memory*

How can you beat the competition vying for the same brain space of your learners?

o   Maximize all the components of working memory.
o   Minimize cognitive load.
o   Marry new knowledge to prior knowledge.

In the next chapter, we'll look at *Principle Five: Durability ... Strengthen Long-Term Memory.*

* * *

APPLICATION

1. Try to draw a picture that visualizes the three types of memory.
2. Why is working memory so important? What are the two channels of working memory?
3. In your own words, define cognitive load.
4. Evaluate a recent talk and ask yourself how you could might re-write and/or deliver it to reduce cognitive load.

Check out the website for downloadable tools at
www.charlesstone.com/TEDfreebies

8

Principle Five: Durability ... Stimulate Long-Term Memory

We soon forget what we have not deeply thought about.
—Marcel Proust, French Novelist

Chapter Big Idea: Principle Five—*Durability ... Stimulate Long-Term Memory* answers the question, *How can you make your message stick in the minds of your audience?* Three key practices will help you apply this principle:

1. Concentrate on enhancing recall.
2. Choose sticky techniques.
3. Create "Aha!" moments.

It was a pleasant walk in the woods of the Jura Mountains for Georges and his dog one summer morning in 1941. After their walks, George de Mestral, an engineer and entrepreneur, would often pull several burs of the cocklebur flowering plant from his trousers and from his dog's fur. On this particular day, the tenacity of the burs piqued his interest. He took a closer look and examined them under a microscope. He noticed small hooks on the burrs made them easily adhere to his pants and his dog's hair. He wondered if he could make something useful from this discovery.

Eight years and much research later, he was able to mimic the natural attachment from the burrs with two pieces of fabric with thousands of hooks and loops. This became the ubiquitous household item we now call Velcro (from the French words "velours" for color and "crochet" for hook) that has revolutionized the fastener industry. He began to commercially produce the product with a company he formed in 1959.

I liken long-term memory to Velcro because both are *sticky*. For learning to actually occur, it must "stick"' in long-term memory, like Velcro, and we must be able to retrieve it. That's what I'll explain in this chapter on durability and stimulating long-term memory.

* * *

PRACTICE ONE: CONCENTRATE ON ENHANCING RECALL

Every communicator should aim for durable learning—learning that sticks in long-term memory that can later be recalled. The saying, "Easy come, easy go," holds true for learning and memory as well. If learning is too easy, little gets learned. Leaning does not reach a stable state and stay there without effort on our part. It needs reinforcement or it fades.

However, if we incorporate recall experiences in our talks that make it a bit hard to recall the material (called desirable difficulty), durable learning will more likely occur. When our listeners must work harder to dig out a memory, understand it, puzzle over it, or make sense of it, they learn better. It's also called "effort after meaning."[227] This process limits simple storage in working memory and forces other relevant circuits to work harder, thus deepening the memory.[228]

But, it must not be too difficult. Not all difficulty is desirable. The goal of desirable difficulty is to make it a bit harder to recall learned material. Communicators must match the difficulty to the learner, making the challenge manageable but not impossible. You're after struggle, not failure. And the more often we recall, the more elaborate memory traces we create which connect that information to other content to improve recall.

A husband-and-wife neuroscience team, Bjork and Bjork, developed the concept of desirable difficulty. It explains how retrieving information (i.e., testing yourself) helps you learn it better. And when we have to exert effort to retrieve information, learning strengthens.[229] Our brains retain what they work harder to obtain.

Although it may seem counterintuitive, forgetting is necessary for remembering. We must forget in order to learn.[230] Forgetting deepens learning because it helps the brain filter out distracting and unnecessary information and strengthen recall of what's important. Memories don't exist on opposite spectrums, totally forgotten to perfectly remembered. Rather,

---

[227] Hardiman, Kindle e-book loc. 2379.

[228] Dehaene, p. 218.

[229] Robert A. Bjork and Elizabeth Ligon Bjork, "A New Theory of Disuse and an Old Theory of Stimulus Fluctuation," in *Essays in Honor of William K. Estes, Vol. 1: From Learning Theory to Connectionist Theory; Vol. 2: From Learning Processes to Cognitive Processes* (Hillsdale, NJ, US: Lawrence Erlbaum Associates, Inc, 1992), 35–67.

[230] Veronica Yan, "Retrieval Strength Vs. Storage Strength — The Learning Scientists," accessed February 14, 2020, https://www.learningscientists.org/blog/2016/5/10-1.

they can be described with two components, retrieval strength and storage strength. This is called the theory of disuse.[231]

Dr. Carole Yue explains the concept in this way, "Any item you encode into your memory can be described by two characteristics: storage strength and retrieval strength. Storage strength is a general measure of how well learned that item is, while retrieval strength measures how accessible the item is at that time. Storage strength increases monotonically—the more you are exposed to an item, the stronger the storage strength gets. One important thing to note is that storage strength does not have a direct effect on memory performance; the probability that you will be able to reproduce something from memory (e.g., a name or phone number) depends almost entirely on its retrieval strength."

She also explains that the very act of retrieving something from memory enhances retrieval strength, and the more difficult it is to retrieve it (desirable difficulty), the stronger the memory becomes. She says, "The more you forget something, the better you ultimately remember it!" So, a little forgetting helps us recall better. And that's the goal we should set for our talks—that our learners will be able to recall in the future what we intend for them to recall and act upon.

Jesus knew how to strengthen recall. He mastered what William Barclay calls the "unforgettable epigram"—a phrase that, "lodges in the mind and stays there, refusing to be forgotten."[232]

---

[231] Elizabeth Bjork and Robert Bjork, "Making Things Hard on Yourself, but in a Good Way: Creating Desirable Difficulties to Enhance Learning," *Psychology and the Real World: Essays Illustrating Fundamental Contributions to Society*, January 1, 2011, 56–64.
[232] William Barclay, *The Mind of Jesus* (San Francisco: HarperOne, 1976), p. 92-93.

The next practice, choose sticky techniques, gives several ideas on how to maximize recall.

* * *

PRACTICE TWO: CHOOSE STICKY TECHNIQUES

In one extensive study, researchers examined 10 different learning techniques to evaluate how well they result in durable learning.[233] They based their study on criteria that included evaluating if they work for different students regardless of material studied and if they work in different learning environments regardless of how they were tested.

Of the 10 learning techniques, these showed the best effect on learning: retrieval practice (testing) which showed the most benefit, distributed practice which showed the second-best benefit (spacing learning out over time versus cramming), interleaved practice (mixing up content of material, ABCABC versus AABBCC), elaboration, and self-explanation. I'll explain these in the pages that follow.

Learners generally prefer other techniques that come more easily. Fast learning techniques like re-reading material, highlighting, and cramming[234] give a sense of familiarity with the material, yet they don't result in durable learning. They simply give an "illusion of fluency," also called the "illusion of knowing." Because someone can recall something the next

---

[233] John Dunlosky et al., "Improving Students' Learning With Effective Learning Techniques: Promising Directions From Cognitive and Educational Psychology," *Psychological Science in the Public Interest* 14, no. 1 (January 2013): 4–58, https://doi.org/10.1177/1529100612453266.

[234] Henry L. Roediger and Mary A. Pyc, "Inexpensive Techniques to Improve Education: Applying Cognitive Psychology to Enhance Educational Practice," *Journal of Applied Research in Memory and Cognition* 1, no. 4 (December 1, 2012): 242–48, https://doi.org/10.1016/j.jarmac.2012.09.002.

day, it makes them think they really know it, when in reality, they don't. They are only *familiar* with the material. They have not really learned it, and after a few days, they probably won't be able to recall it. Fast learning promotes fast forgetting, yet slow learning promotes more long-lasting learning and greater retention. Fast learning does not allow enough time for the brain to make more neural connections and associations.

Jesus used several sticky techniques that promoted durable learning. "Almost anything could become grist for Jesus' mill."[235] He used parables with hidden meanings to force His listeners to think. The late Dallas Seminary professor, Dr. Roy Zuck, noted that Jesus used "lecturing, discussions, questions, answers to questions, brief statements, conversations or dialogues, stories or parables, disputes, demonstrations, quotations, maxims, challenges, rebukes, comments, riddles, arguments, and even silence."[236] All of these were powerful tools that Jesus used to imbed learning.

Testing

The word "test" evokes anxiety in almost every student. Testing usually means grades. Testing certainly helps assess how much we know at the time, and it may or may not reflect durable learning. But research has discovered that testing itself is a significant way to enhance learning.[237] It's called the *testing effect* which results in better recall in students than

---

[235] Mr. Robert J. Banks, *Reenvisioning Theological Education: Exploring a Missional Alternative to Current Models* (Wm. B. Eerdmans Publishing, 1999), p. 106.
[236] *Zuck,* p. 165.
[237] Henry L. Roediger and Andrew C. Butler, "The Critical Role of Retrieval Practice in Long-Term Retention," *Trends in Cognitive Sciences* 15, no. 1 (January 2011): 20–27, https://doi.org/10.1016/j.tics.2010.09.003, p. 21.

when they simply re-read their books or notes. Baddeley and associates write how testing enhances memory:

> Restudy strengthens only the memory traces formed at initial study. When learners apply retrieval effort during testing, however, this strengthens the memory trace formed at initial study AND leads to the formation of a second memory trace. Thus, testing involving retrieval effort generally promotes superior memory to restudy because it promotes the acquisition of two memory traces rather than just one. It is important to note that the above predictions apply only when feedback (provision of the correct answers) occurs during testing. If participants fail to supply the correct answers for any items during testing (and they receive no feedback), then no second memory trace will be formed for those items.[238]

Quality feedback is a key to durable learning,[239] and we'll cover that later.

There are two general kinds of tests—summative and formative. Most of us have taken summative tests, those that indicate how much we know at that moment that results in a grade. Formative testing, however, is different. It can actually enhance learning by informing us about what we still need to know. It helps form new memories rather than judge what we know. Such assessments can "re-heat" related neural networks, activating prior knowledge to enhance curiosity in learners.

---

[238] Baddeley, Eysenck, and Anderson, p. 553.
[239] John Hattie and Helen Timperley, "The Power of Feedback," *Review of Educational Research* 77, no. 1 (March 1, 2007): 81–112, https://doi.org/10.3102/003465430298487.

Tests given from a formative perspective solidify long-term learning and retention.[240] By retrieving the information and reconstructing it, learning deepens. And repeated testing of the same material over time enhances learning better than repeated study of the material.[241] Of course, learners must begin with study to become sufficiently familiar with the material.

One method of formative testing is called generation. It's asking a question before you give the answer, forcing the learner to attempt an answer to the question. Trying to answer a question when you don't know the answer makes you more receptive to the new learning that will follow. It also helps learners experience "aha!" moments (below) which drive learning deeper. Even if your learners answer incorrectly, it's okay as long as you soon give them the correct answers. Even guessing at a correct answer increases the chance a learner will get the answer correctly when tested at a later time.[242]

Generation works because it forces learners to process information more deeply and helps them relate new information to existing information already stored in long-term memory, which enhances durable learning in turn.

Author Peter Brown notes, "One explanation for this effect is the idea that as you cast about for a solution, retrieving related knowledge from memory, you strengthen the route to a gap in your learning even before the answer is provided to fill it and, when you do fill it, connections are made to the related material that is fresh in your mind from the effort."[243] Their

---

[240] Roediger and Butler, "The Critical Role of Retrieval Practice in Long-Term Retention."

[241] Roediger and Butler.

[242] Didau, p. 262-264.

[243] Peter C. Brown, Henry L. Roediger III, and Mark A. McDaniel, *Make It Stick: The Science of Successful Learning*, 1 edition (Cambridge, Massachusetts: Belknap Press: An Imprint of Harvard University Press, 2014), Kindle e-book loc. 1214.

"casting about" may strengthen the connections between schemas to aid learning. And the stronger those connections, the greater the learning. It might be that knowing what we don't know increases learning.

When you create your talks, consider incorporating different kinds of tests, pre-tests, post-tests, pop quizzes, and even self-testing at the end of a teaching session by asking your learners to test themselves on what they learned.

Jesus often tested His followers with questions, a common practice used in that day to discern how well students had learned the lesson being taught.[244] For example, in Matthew 16, Jesus asked His disciples who others said He was and then asked them who they thought He was.

Estimates of the number of questions recorded in the Gospels, depending on how you count them, range from 110 to 310.[245] And in Jesus' most famous sermon, the Sermon on the Mount (Matt. 5), He asks 15 questions and another six that His hearers might ask. In fact, the first recorded words of Jesus were when He was 12, and He posed two questions to Mary and Joseph, "'Why were you searching for me?' he asked. 'Didn't you know I had to be in my Father's house?'" (Luke 2:49)

He always used questions with a purpose—to rouse interest, confront His critics, probe for motives, push for faith, promote reflection, prick the conscience, etc.[246] He never used them as fillers or to simply promote good discussion, and the Gospels record 20 individuals and 12 groups who even asked Jesus questions.[247] Your communication setting may allow your learners to ask you questions. About the questions others

---

[244] Wasukundi.

[245] Zuck, p. 237.

[246] Zuck, p. 241.

[247] Zuck, p. 278.

asked Jesus, He always responded with respect and attentiveness, never calling any question unnecessary or foolish.

One reminder, however. Jesus did not assess His disciples fit for ministry by the "quality of their term papers or their performance in examinations whether written or oral."[248] Likewise, communicators must not let testing, although it drives learning deeper, become the end-all measure of success.

Educational researchers Henry L. Roediger and Mary A. Pyc note 10 benefits of testing.[249] Although all of these benefits may not apply in your communication setting, some of them can apply to any setting:

Benefit 1: The testing effect—retrieval aids later retention.

Benefit 2: Testing identifies gaps in knowledge, and pre-tests can aid learning. Even wrong answers, if given immediate feedback, can enhance learning because it primes us to notice important information later on.

Benefit 3: Testing causes students to learn more from the next study episode.

Benefit 4: Testing produces better organization of knowledge.

Benefit 5: Testing improves transfer of knowledge to new contexts.

Benefit 6: Testing can facilitate retrieval of material that was not tested.

Benefit 7: Testing improves metacognitive monitoring [thinking about thinking].

---

[248] Ferdinando, "Jesus, the Theological Educator."

[249] Henry Roediger, Adam Putnam, and Megan Sumeracki, "Ten Benefits of Testing and Their Applications to Educational Practice," in *Psychology of Learning and Motivation - PSYCH LEARN MOTIV-ADV RES TH*, vol. 55, 2011, 1–36, https://doi.org/10.1016/B978-0-12-387691-1.00001-6.

Benefit 8: Testing prevents interference from prior material when learning new material.

Benefit 9: Testing provides feedback to instructors.

Benefit 10: Frequent testing encourages students to study.

Testing: Feedback and Evaluation

One of the best ways to maximize the effect from formative testing (and learning in general), is to provide timely feedback.[250] That is, not only should you correct wrong answers, but you should also give your learners the right answers. However, feedback given too often or too quickly can cause learners to over-depend on it and thus stifle learning.[251] Helpful feedback should provide clarity (correct the errors), motivate learners to increase their effort, and help them aspire to greater challenge.

Providing correct feedback with a bit of delay is even more effective than immediate feedback, perhaps due to the spacing effect discussed below (spacing out learning).[252] However, you don't want to wait too long because the effect of feedback on performance fades over time.[253] Feedback provided closer to the time of learning makes the greatest positive difference.[254]

The most effective feedback should include these qualities: timely (given soon after assessment), specific and descriptive (highlighting explicit strengths and weaknesses),

---

[250] Mayer, p. 458.

[251] Didau, p. 277.

[252] Roediger and Butler, "The Critical Role of Retrieval Practice in Long-Term Retention."

[253] Keri L. Kettle and Gerald Häubl, "Motivation by Anticipation: Expecting Rapid Feedback Enhances Performance," *Psychological Science* 21, no. 4 (April 1, 2010): 545–47, https://doi.org/10.1177/0956797610363541.

[254] Harold Pashler et al., "When Does Feedback Facilitate Learning of Words?," *Journal of Experimental Psychology. Learning, Memory, and Cognition* 31, no. 1 (January 2005): 3–8, https://doi.org/10.1037/0278-7393.31.1.3.

understandable and actionable (learner friendly), and allowing learners to actually use it to help change their thinking about the subject.

If you want to maximize the testing effect, give "free recall" tests. After a talk or lesson, ask your learners to write down everything they can recall for two minutes. Research indicates that this kind of testing results in even greater learning and recall.[255]

So, from a brain perspective, why does repeated testing improve our learning and memory? One possible reason is testing forces our brains to retrieve the information which creates more routes by which we can later retrieve the memory (like multiple routes you might take to drive home from work each day). Another theory is that retrieval through testing takes effort, and that effort helps the memory get reprocessed which strengthens it, making it more durable and flexible for future use. One other theory revolves around the neurotransmitter dopamine. When we learn something new or novel, the brain produces dopamine, and the act of retrieving that memory releases more dopamine which solidifies the learning.[256]

In summary, testing enhances learning when these four parts are included: effort from the learner, multiple tests, testing over intervals (spacing), and feedback.[257]

[255] Katherine A. Rawson and Amanda Zamary, "Why Is Free Recall Practice More Effective than Recognition Practice for Enhancing Memory? Evaluating the Relational Processing Hypothesis," *Journal of Memory and Language* 105 (April 1, 2019): 141–52, https://doi.org/10.1016/j.jml.2019.01.002.
[256] Roediger and Butler, "The Critical Role of Retrieval Practice in Long-Term Retention."
[257] Roediger and Butler.

Spacing

Spacing simply means to space out learning over time versus cramming. [258] Spacing within a single talk might be a challenge, but if you have multiple sessions (i.e., sermons series, a full-day training session, a multi-day class), spacing can foster durable learning. Spacing is like watering your flowers. It's better to water them a bit each day than to drown them with an overabundance once a week.

One study by Carol-Anne Moulton illustrated the long-term benefits from spacing.[259] Thirty-eight surgical residents were trained to perform a specific type of microscopic surgery that required they connect tiny blood vessels together. Half of the residents received the standard training, all four sessions in one day. The other half received the four sessions one week apart for four weeks.

They all got the same training, but one group received theirs spaced out over time. A month later, they were all asked to perform this surgery on rats. Guess which group completed the surgeries most successfully? The ones who received spaced training. Some in the day-long training were not successful. Also, experts rated the surgeries from the residents who received spaced training as superior to the other group's surgeries.

Spacing helps avoid the illusion of knowing. For example, simply re-reading material may increase familiarity but does not necessarily increase recall ability. Recognition of material does not mean you can recall it. Familiarity does not equal

---

[258] "A Powerful Way to Improve Learning and Memory," https://www.apa.org, accessed July 12, 2019, https://www.apa.org/science/about/psa/2016/06/learning-memory.

[259] Carol-Anne E. Moulton et al., "Teaching Surgical Skills: What Kind of Practice Makes Perfect?," *Annals of Surgery* 244, no. 3 (September 2006): 400–409, https://doi.org/10.1097/01.sla.0000234808.85789.6a.

mastery. In fact, familiarity and recall are stored in different parts of the brain. Learners generally don't prefer spacing because it feels they aren't progressing as fast as they might feel from massed learning.

Why does spacing work? The verdict is still out, but one reason is because the brain gets bored easily. It becomes progressively less interested in information that is repeated over and over in succession. Spacing apparently keeps interest up.[260] Another reason may be that spacing allows some forgetting, which, as I mentioned earlier, is not all bad. Forgetting can filter out unnecessary information. Later practice and recall can deepen learning by helping learners realize the gaps in their knowledge that require more study. Finally, spacing learning on different days and/or in different contexts can help create more cues and thus more neural pathways that aid recall and learning (like practicing your tennis serve on successive days with different weather conditions). One study noted that spaced retrieval actually produces a chemical change in our brains (production of a protein) that massed learning or cramming does not.[261]

"The rule of thumb is to review the information at intervals of approximately 20 percent of the desired memory duration—for instance, rehearse after two months if you want a memory to last about ten months."[262]

---

[260] Benedict Carey, *How We Learn: The Surprising Truth About When, Where, and Why It Happens*, Reprint edition (New York, NY: Random House Trade Paperbacks, 2015), p. 74.

[261] Takehito Okamoto et al., "Role of Cerebellar Cortical Protein Synthesis in Transfer of Memory Trace of Cerebellum-Dependent Motor Learning," *Journal of Neuroscience* 31, no. 24 (June 15, 2011): 8958–66, https://doi.org/10.1523/JNEUROSCI.1151-11.2011.

[262] Dehaene, p. 218.

Interleaving

Interleaving is mixing new-but-related material with previously learned material. It's like what coaches do when they mix weight training with endurance training in a daily practice routine. At the brain level, this is how it works, "If we interleave the rehearsal of previously stored information with the rehearsal of new information, then we can make synaptic changes that incorporate both memories simultaneously. But that requires regularly rehearsing previously stored information."[263]

Interleaving may work for several reasons. It helps learners prepare for the unexpected, distinguish between different concepts, understand the gist of your topic, and choose different strategies to problem solve, mirroring real life.[264] And because the brain does not know what is coming next, interleaving forces it to work a bit harder. Gradual consolidation through interleaving benefits long-term memory because it incorporates new information without overwriting existing memories.[265] Memories that are interleaved over time last longer.

In one study,[266] two groups of children practiced throwing bean bags at a target. Half the children only practiced throwing the bean bag into the target three feet away. The other half practiced throwing the bags at targets from various distances. After training, the kids were tested, and the children who threw at varying distances performed consistently

[263] Dr Thad A Polk, *The Learning Brain*, The Great Courses (Chantilly, VA: The Great Courses, 2018), p. 57.

[264] Weinstein, Sumeracki, and Caviglioli, *Understanding How We Learn*.

[265] McClelland, McNaughton, and O'Reilly, "Why There Are Complementary Learning Systems in the Hippocampus and Neocortex."

[266] Robert Kerr and Bernard Booth, "Specific and Varied Practice of Motor Skill," *Perceptual and Motor Skills* 46, no. 2 (April 1, 1978): 395–401, https://doi.org/10.1177/003151257804600201.

better than the children who threw from only three feet. This finding implies that interleaving information can increase your ability to use knowledge in different settings in real life.

Jesus often did this because He made "deeper connections across different disciplines that he taught: Healing of soul and body, feeding of hungry crowds, authority and leadership, gender, respect and equality for all human beings, forgiveness and mercy (the Samaritan, prodigal son, etc.)."[267]

Imagine trekking through a deep jungle. It's difficult to carve a path because none exists. But each time you take that path, it becomes easier. Getting all the information at once would be like taking a single trip whereas interleaving would be like taking the path many times. The more times you travel the path, the better the chance you'll find it again.

Both spaced retrieval (testing) and interleaving place a time delay between exposure to new material and recall which enhances learning.[268] Sleep can also aid this process because our brain consolidates the prior day's memories during sleep by rehearsing them, thus consolidating them.[269]

Elaboration, Reflection, and Generation

Elaboration is helping your listeners deepen learning by connecting prior knowledge to new knowledge. It's guiding them to ask the *how* and *why* questions so they add something to memory by thinking more deeply about it. Elaboration is a major pillar of the modern educational theory, constructivism, which proposes learners best learn when they build upon

[267] Wasukundi.
[268] Roediger and Pyc, "Inexpensive Techniques to Improve Education."
[269] Daoyun Ji and Matthew A. Wilson, "Coordinated Memory Replay in the Visual Cortex and Hippocampus during Sleep," *Nature Neuroscience* 10, no. 1 (January 2007): 100–107, https://doi.org/10.1038/nn1825.

their own understanding and knowledge to deepen it. When we process information more deeply this way, in contrast to shallow processing, we remember better. Deep processing includes several specific techniques: reflection, *why* and *how* questions, examples, metaphors, stories, and generation.

Here are some practical ways to build these ideas into your talks:[270]

1. Have them revisit old memories.
2. Help them make new connections between concepts.
3. Guide them to think about something they learned in the past.
4. Help them find new meaning in a concept.
5. Get them to compare and contrast two different ideas.
6. Have them paraphrase.
7. Encourage note-taking.

Note-taking simultaneously engages multiple memory pathways, makes us self-reflect, forces us to synthesize by including some information and excluding other information, and integrates many brain areas.[271]

Hand-written notes are even more effective for recall than taking notes with a computer.[272] [273] When possible, provide "guided notes" where your listeners can fill in the blanks for the most important points of

---

[270] Simon, Kindle e-book loc. 983.

[271] Tokuhama-Espinosa, *Making Classrooms Better,* Kindle e-book loc 4300.

[272] "Handwriting vs. Typing: How to Choose the Best Method to Take Notes—Effectiviology," accessed October 14, 2019, https://effectiviology.com/handwriting-vs-typing-how-to-take-notes/.

[273] Pam A. Mueller and Daniel M. Oppenheimer, "The Pen Is Mightier Than the Keyboard: Advantages of Longhand Over Laptop Note Taking," *Psychological Science* 25, no. 6 (June 1, 2014): 1159–68, https://doi.org/10.1177/0956797614524581.

your talk. Guided notes will produce deeper learning than what unstructured note-taking provides.[274]

8. Have them summarize and synthesize your material to get the main idea.

9. Ask questions.

Questions are powerful communication tools. When we're asked a question, it literally takes over our brain, triggering a mental reflex called "instinctive elaboration."[275] A question about a future decision increases the chances they will make that decision. These kinds of questions force deeper thinking and require more than a simple "Yes" or "No" answer.

Keep in mind that when you ask a question, whether you want an audible response or not, it's important to give your learners ample time to answer, at least five seconds. If you wait that long, you'll most likely get more and deeper responses.

At the end of a talk, give time for your learners to answer the three questions below,[276] and if your teaching occurs over several time slots, encourage them to keep a journal with each session's responses to the questions. *What new thing did you learn about (_____) today? How does this connect to what you already know about (_____)? How can you use this new knowledge in the future?*

---

[274] Moira Konrad, Laurice Joseph, and Elisha Eveleigh, "A Meta-Analytic Review of Guided Notes," *Education and Treatment of Children* 32 (January 1, 2009): 421–44, https://doi.org/10.1353/etc.0.0066.

[275] David Hoffeld, "Want To Know What Your Brain Does When It Hears A Question?," Fast Company, February 21, 2017, https://www.fastcompany.com/3068341/want-to-know-what-your-brain-does-when-it-hears-a-question.

[276] Sousa, p. 185.

Questions help learners reflect which enhances long-term memory, as a study from Harvard University discovered, "Employees who spent the last 15 minutes of each day of their training period writing and reflecting on what they had learned did 23% better in the final training test than other employees."[277]
10. Help them compare and contrast.[278]

Jesus modeled elaboration when He asked the disciples questions, expecting them to build upon prior understanding. He stirred "introspection, deep learning, and active participation with conversion of the heart and redemption being at the center of its primary goal."[279] Jesus didn't limit His teaching to lecture only, even though His teaching amazed people. Rather, He invited people to actively participate in learning. Lecturing alone, no matter how polished, will not foster durable learning. Unfortunately, people think they learn more from a lecture than from their active participation.[280]

Mark 8:27-29 illustrates one way Jesus used questions, "Jesus and his disciples went on to the villages around Caesarea Philippi. On the way he asked them, 'Who do people say I am?' They replied, 'Some say John the Baptist; others say

---

[277] Giada Di Stefano et al., "Making Experience Count: The Role of Reflection in Individual Learning," SSRN Scholarly Paper (Rochester, NY: Social Science Research Network, June 14, 2016), https://papers.ssrn.com/abstract=2414478.
[278] Robert J. Marzano, Debra J. Pickering, and Jane E. Pollock, *Classroom Instruction That Works: Research-Based Strategies for Increasing Student Achievement* (Association for Supervision and Curriculum Development, 1703 North Beauregard Street, Alexandria, VA 22311-1714; Tel: 703-578-9600 or 800-933-2723; Fax: 703-575-5400; E-mail: member@ascd, 2001).
[279] Wasukundi.
[280] Louis Deslauriers et al., "Measuring Actual Learning versus Feeling of Learning in Response to Being Actively Engaged in the Classroom," *Proceedings of the National Academy of Sciences* 116, no. 39 (September 24, 2019): 19251–57, https://doi.org/10.1073/pnas.1821936116.

Elijah; and still others, one of the prophets.' 'But what about you?' he asked. 'Who do you say I am?'"

He also modeled these techniques through His parables which required deep reflection and synthesis (i.e., the parable of the landowner in Matt. 20:1-15, the parable of the ten virgins in Matt. 25:1-13, the unforgiving servant in Matt. 18:23-35). "He never did all the thinking."[281] Rather, He wanted His followers to think for themselves.

Jesus invited people to go on a journey with Him. In one powerful illustration in Luke 10, Jesus explained the implications of eternal life to an expert in the law. The expert asked Jesus to define who his neighbor was because Jesus had said, "Love your neighbor as yourself." Jesus could have answered him with a succinct, crisp, "just the facts" answer. Instead, He took the expert on a journey of self-discovery as He told the story of what we call the Good Samaritan. By telling the story, instead of answering for him, Jesus made him decide for himself who a real neighbor was which drove much deeper the conviction about his wrong attitude. Jesus would often tell parables this way, not immediately explaining them until later in order to force His listeners to consider their meaning.

* * *

PRACTICE THREE: CREATE "AHA!" MOMENTS

Insight ("Aha!" moments) is a solution to a problem that recombines what we know in a new and fresh way. It relates to creativity. Rather than solving a problem analytically when we focus our attention outwardly on the problem, insight occurs when we turn our attention inward and become less focused.

---

[281] DeMent, "Principles and Methods of the Master Teacher."

This inward focus can help us experience a sudden "Aha!" solution. This historical illustration about insight describes the "Aha!" process well.

We use the word "eureka," attributed to Archimedes (c. 287 BC—c. 212 BC), to describe an "Aha!" moment, a flash of insight we sometimes get. As a brilliant scientist in antiquity, Archimedes is known for a story about his inventing a method to determine an object's volume. A goldsmith had forged a crown of gold for the then current king, King Hiero II. He was concerned, however, that the goldsmith has substituted silver, a cheaper metal, for some of the gold. He asked Archimedes to find the truth without melting the crown. This stumped Archimedes until a flash of insight appeared to him.

One day as he took a bath, he noticed the water level rise as he stepped in. Suddenly, he realized that by making a few mathematical calculations, he could use water-volume displacement from the crown to determine if it was indeed made of pure gold. In his excitement (as legend suggests), he ran naked into the streets crying, "Eureka, Eureka!" which means in Greek, "I have found it." Thus, we use the word "eureka" to describe insight. Through this insight, he discovered the goldsmith had indeed substituted silver for some of the crown's gold.

Archimedes had discovered an insight in a moment when he wasn't even thinking about the problem. When we get a "eureka" or an "Aha!" insight, we just know the answer without actually knowing how we got it. The insight doesn't come piece by piece, but usually all at once.

Researchers who study insight use a word game called Compound Remote Associate (CRA) problems. Study participants try to create three two-word phrases from three words that could share a common word. For example, consider these three words: barrel, root, and belly. What two-word phrases can you create that share a common word? Participants often use the word beer to create beer barrel, root beer, and beer belly. After they solve the problem, they press a button to indicate how they solved it, either logically or with an "Aha!" insight. Using both EEG and fMRI, neuroscientists then examine their brain functioning[282] to learn what happens during insight.

Through these studies, researchers discovered a process that occurs in our brain when it receives an insight. First, our brain is at rest in what is called the default mode. We may be daydreaming or our minds may be wandering. fMRI studies show that at this stage, the alpha wave (the wave active when the brain idles during daydreaming and relaxation) spikes. This indicates that our brain is visually gating,[283] reducing the visual input it's processing to reduce distractions.

This is in contrast to the brain's dominant wave, the beta wave, active during visual focus and alertness. The alpha wave shows the part of our brain behind our eyebrows is more active prior to an insight. This part of the brain, the anterior cingulate cortex, "lights up" when it senses conflict. This makes us more aware of competing alternatives and enhances our predisposition to switch between difference solutions,[284] potentially creating an insight. That is, if one solution doesn't work, the brain will try another. This part of our brain helps orchestrate attention since it is so highly connected to the rest of the brain.

---

[282] Mark Jung-Beeman, A Collier, and John Kounios, "How Insight Happens: Learning from the Brain," *Neuroleadership Journal*, no. 1 (2008): 20–25.

[283] Simone Sandkühler and Joydeep Bhattacharya, "Deconstructing Insight: EEG Correlates of Insightful Problem Solving," *PLoS ONE* 3, no. 1 (January 23, 2008): e1459, https://doi.org/10.1371/journal.pone.0001459.

[284] Jung-Beeman, Collier, and Kounios, "How Insight Happens: Learning from the Brain."

Finally, at the moment an insight occurs, the gamma wave spikes.[285] A gamma wave, the fastest brain wave, sweeps across the entire brain 40 times per second to bring our brain to attention, much like how a conductor synchronizes an orchestra when they raise the baton. The gamma band activity indicates new brain maps are being formed, the insight. And when that happens, it literally feels good because neurotransmitters are released. As the insight occurs at the point of gamma synchrony, right hemisphere activity also increases to help us make connections with subtle associations we might have otherwise missed. The brain's right hemisphere, which process information more intuitively and holistically, apparently drives the insight process (the material above adapted from *Brain Savvy Leaders* by Charles Stone, ©2015 Abingdon Press. Used by Permission. All rights reserved).

Jesus masterfully created "Aha!" moments in the minds of His listeners. On one occasion He broke all of the current social protocols by talking to a woman who was a Samaritan (John 4). In that day, a Jewish rabbi would never do that. But Jesus did because He knew this woman's heart. As she approached the common water well in the village of Sychar, He began a conversation with her, using water as a metaphor. During the conversation, He paralleled physical water with living water which created an "Aha!" moment in her as she requested this living water. As the conversation continued and Jesus pointed to her illicit background (with great grace), it evoked in her a recognition that He was the Messiah. Later, when she traveled back to town, she shared this encounter

---

[285] John Kounios et al., "The Prepared Mind: Neural Activity Prior to Problem Presentation Predicts Subsequent Solution by Sudden Insight," *Psychological Science* 17, no. 10 (October 2006): 882–90, https://doi.org/10.1111/j.1467-9280.2006.01798.x.

with others. Jesus helped evoke in her some "Aha!" moments using common objects, questions, and metaphors.

"Aha!" moments relate to creativity. Consider the following ways to encourage these moments in your learners:[286]

1. Provide a wealth of information in the area you are teaching.
2. Encourage learners to provide multiple options to open-ended prompts.
3. Pose questions or problems that might have more than one correct answer.
4. When learners give solutions, ask them to consider implications and implementation.
5. Provide group work.
6. Offer novel relationships and ask learners to create ideas that exemplify those relationships.
7. Encourage learners to find novel relationships between unrelated ideas.
8. Use external items like worksheets, visuals, or bulleted summaries that relate to the content you are teaching.

I wrote earlier about models in our minds called schemas (neural manila folders) that help us make sense of how the world works. When we learn something new, our brain tries to work the new stuff into a current schema. As you speak and use appropriate tools in your communicator's toolbox, you are helping your learners make connections to those existing schemas so that the new knowledge, "snaps into place with a satisfying *aha!*"[287]

---

[286] Gregory et al., "Building Creative Thinking in the Classroom."
[287] Anderson, p. 76.

* * *

In summary, *Principle Five: Durability ... Stimulate Long-term Memory* means that we use communication techniques to help drive learning into long-term memory, thus enhancing durable learning. I suggested three ways to do this. First, focus on enhancing recall. Learning has not happened unless the learner can recall. Second, choose sticky techniques. Third, create, "Aha!" moments.

Principle Five: *Durability ... Stimulate Long-Term Memory*

How can you make your message stick in the minds of your audience?

o   Concentrate on enhancing recall.
o   Choose sticky techniques.
o   Create "Aha!" moments.

In the next chapter, we'll look at *Principle Six: Emotion ... Engage the heart.*

* * *

APPLICATION

1. How could you incorporate a test into your next talk?
2. In your setting, what might feedback look like to your learners after you give a talk?
3. How might spacing work in a single talk?
4. When have you experienced an "Aha!" moment when listening to someone's talk? What made it so?

Check out the website for downloadable tools at
www.charlesstone.com/TEDfreebies

9

Principle Six: Emotion ...
Engage the Heart

It is literally neurobiologically impossible to build memories, engage complex thoughts, or make meaningful decisions without emotion.[288]

—Mary Helen Immordino-Yang

Setting the emotional climate for learning may be the most important task a teacher embarks on each day.[289]

—Mariale Hardiman

Although many of us may think of ourselves as thinking creatures that feel, biologically we are feeling creatures that think.[290]

—Jill Bolt Taylor

---

[288] Immordino-Yang, p. 17.
[289] Mariale M. Hardiman, *The Brain-Targeted Teaching Model for 21st-Century Schools*, 1 edition (Thousand Oaks, Calif: Corwin, 2012), Kindle e-book loc. 1015.
[290] Jill Bolte Taylor, *My Stroke of Insight: A Brain Scientist's Personal Journey*, 1 Reprint edition (New York: Plume, 2009), p. 19.

> **Chapter Big Idea: Principle Six—***Emotion ... Engage the heart* answers the question, *How can you help your learners feel your message?* Three key practices will help you apply this principle:
>
> 1. Leverage emotional learning.
> 2. Limit cognitive dissonance.
> 3. Lead with well-placed stories.

The image is forever seared into my memory.

We lived in California at the time, and a phone call startled us awake. My son Josh was on the other end, calling from college. He said, "Dad, turn the TV on. I think it's Armageddon!"

You can image the fear I felt as I heard his words. I quickly grabbed the remote and turned the TV on. Within seconds, I saw a video of what I thought was a movie at first. The video showed a passenger jet flying into a tall building and exploding. I couldn't quite make sense of it until I read the scrolling words below, "Jets hit Twin Towers. Pentagon hit. Many dead."

Over the next few minutes, I began to understand what was unfolding. It was September 11, 2001, when terrorists hijacked planes and attacked the United States.

The emotion of the moment seared the experience into my memory—where I was and what I felt at that moment in history. You can probably recall where you were when "9/11" occurred. Psychologists call these memories *flashbulb* memories, and although we think we can recall such events accurately, research shows we actually don't recall them as accurately as we think.[291] Nevertheless, these experiences illustrate how emotion impacts memory and learning. Fortunately, all of life's experiences don't rise to the emotional level of "9/11," but research tells us emotion impacts the mental processes of perception, attention, learning, memory, reasoning, and problem solving.[292]

Emotion can powerfully enhance learning. When we feel emotionally aroused, we narrow the spotlight of our attention to what's most important.[293] We ignore certain things and focus on others. An example of this is what researchers have discovered when someone encounters a person with a gun. They focus their attention on the gun and not on the person holding it. The emotion forces them to narrow the focus of their attention.[294] And focused attention enhances learning and memory, but too much emotion can impair learning. Short-term emotion or stress can actually enhance learning, whereas long-term, chronic stress undermines it.

In this chapter, we'll look at how you can use emotion to enhance your talks.

* * *

---

[291] William Hirst et al., "A Ten-Year Follow-up of a Study of Memory for the Attack of September 11, 2001: Flashbulb Memories and Memories for Flashbulb Events," *Journal of Experimental Psychology: General* 144, no. 3 (2015): 604–23, https://doi.org/10.1037/xge0000055.
[292] Chai M. Tyng et al., "The Influences of Emotion on Learning and Memory," *Frontiers in Psychology* 8 (August 24, 2017), https://doi.org/10.3389/fpsyg.2017.01454.
[293] J. A. Easterbrook, "The Effect of Emotion on Cue Utilization and the Organization of Behavior," *Psychological Review* 66, no. 3 (May 1959): 183–201, https://doi.org/10.1037/h0047707.
[294] Elizabeth Loftus, Geoffrey Loftus, and Jane Messo, "Some Facts about 'Weapon Focus,'" *Law and Human Behavior* 11 (March 1, 1987): 55, https://doi.org/10.1007/BF01044839.

PRACTICE ONE: LEVERAGE EMOTIONAL LEARNING

World renowned neuroscientist Mary Helen Immordino-Yang explains how emotion affects learning and cognition, "The basic premise is that when learning and knowledge are relatively devoid of emotion, when people learn things by 'rote' without internally driven motivation and without a sense of interest or real-world relevance, then it is likely that they won't be able to use what they learn efficiently in the real world."[295]

She also notes, "Although its influence during learning may not be openly visible, emotion stabilizes the direction of a learner's decisions and behaviors over time, helping the learner to steer toward strategies that have worked well in similar situations in the past. In this way, implicit emotional memories are an integral part of learning and thinking."[296] And when people lose their ability to feel emotion, even decision making gets compromised. So, emotion is critical to durable learning, although scientists have not always believed that.

Into the 1980s, scientists generally believed that a top-down cognition process imposed itself on our bodies as the primary influencer of our behavior and learning. Many did not accept that emotions had a strong brain basis. Emotions were seen "like a toddler in a china shop, interfering with the orderly rows of (cognitive) stemware on the shelves."[297] As a result, educators and communicators failed (and some still do) to see that learning does not function as a disembodied process detached from emotion.

However, during this time when cognition was king, scientists began to notice that when certain parts of the brain were

---

[295] Immordino-Yang, Damasio, and Gardner, p. 28.

[296] Immordino-Yang, Damasio, and Gardner, pp. 93-94.

[297] Immordino-Yang, Damasio, and Gardner, p. 29.

damaged, they could not explain changed behavior simply in terms of cognition. They observed that many brain-damaged people could not exercise self-control or make wise decisions. Traditionally, scientists had explained these deficits in terms of the loss of their knowledge base. As they tested these patients, however, they discovered the issue was not a loss of knowledge or logical reasoning, their access to knowledge, or a decrease in IQ. And although these people could explain the social and moral rules that should guide their behavior, they made poor choices, contrary to the behavior they showed before their brain damage. They were insensitive to the emotions of others and oblivious to the consequences of their actions. They could not learn from their mistakes, prior rewards or punishments, or the disapproval of others.[298]

Researchers were able to connect their lost moral and social inhibition to their loss of emotions like guilt, embarrassment, compassion, or empathy. Their emotional processing had been compromised. They weren't able to "perceive and incorporate social feedback in learning."[299] Researchers called these emotion-related processes an "emotional rudder" that guided judgment and action. Although knowledge and logic remained intact in these patients, emotional knowledge that had previously guided their behavior no longer did. Emotional learning (consequences, others' approval or disapproval, etc.) no longer informed healthy decision making. They had lost their ability to emotionally tag behavior.

Now, research informs us that these emotions are not just toddlers in a china shop, but more like "shelves underlying

---

[298] Mary Helen1 Immordino-Yang mhimmordino-yang@post.harvard.edu and Antonio2 Damasio, "We Feel, Therefore We Learn: The Relevance of Affective and Social Neuroscience to Education," *Mind, Brain & Education* 1, no. 1 (March 2007): 3–10, https://doi.org/10.1111/j.1751-228X.2007.00004.x.
[299] Immordino-Yang and Damasio.

the glassware; without them cognition has less support."[300] Emotions are now seen as a "basic form of decision making, a repertoire of know-how and actions that allows people to respond appropriately in different situations."[301]

Emotions overlap cognition and are profoundly linked with thought. They influence our body (i.e., tensing up and increased heart rate when we feel fear) which in turn creates feelings (conscious awareness of the sensations involved in emotions). Our feelings, in turn, influence thinking which influences behavior. Thus, emotions impact learning.

Real-world application of what we learn, called transfer (more on this later), depends on emotion. As Immordino-Yang and Damasio write, "The neurological systems that support decision making generally are the same systems that support social and moral behavior. Without adequate access to emotional, social, and moral feedback, in effect the important elements of culture, learning cannot inform real-world functioning as effectively."[302]

Much research today supports this crucial concept: durable learning is not purely a rational process divorced from emotion but highly influenced by it. Effective communicators must leverage emotional learning.

Yang's research yielded five insights about how emotion relates to learning:[303]

---

[300] Mary Helen1 Immordino-Yang mhimmordino-yang@post.harvard.edu and Antonio2 Damasio, "We Feel, Therefore We Learn: The Relevance of Affective and Social Neuroscience to Education," *Mind, Brain & Education* 1, no. 1 (March 2007): 3–10, https://doi.org/10.1111/j.1751-228X.2007.00004.x.

[301] Immordino-Yang and Damasio, "We Feel, Therefore We Learn."

[302] Immordino-Yang and Damasio.

[303] Immordino-Yang, Damasio, and Gardner, *Emotions, Learning, and the Brain*, pp. 96-99.

1. Emotion guides cognitive learning.
2. Emotional contributions to learning can be conscious or nonconscious.
3. Emotional learning shapes future behavior.
4. Emotion is most effective at facilitating the development of knowledge when it is relevant to the task at hand.
5. Without emotion, learning is impaired.

Emotions clearly play an important role in learning and changing behavior. Learning through a rational process of analyze-think-change rarely changes us. Rather, a durable learning sequence looks more like this: see-feel-change.[304] When you properly use emotion in a talk, you can, "harness (y)our [learners'] attention, dominate their working memory resources, enhance their long-term memory consolidation, and fuel their motivation."[305] And two key neurotransmitters, dopamine and norepinephrine (among others) that help cement learning, increase when emotion is involved.[306]

It's worth noting that emotion is not absolutely required to learn everything or else we'd never learn a lot of what students encounter in school (learning 2+2 is not very emotional). Educational expert Daniel Willingham provides a helpful reminder that learning can still occur when emotion is not present when he writes, "Things that create an emotional reaction will be better remembered, but emotion is not necessary

---

[304] Mezirow and Taylor, p. 10.
[305] Cavanagh, p. 32.
[306] Yadollah Ranjbar-Slamloo and Zeinab Fazlali, "Dopamine and Noradrenaline in the Brain; Overlapping or Dissociate Functions?," *Frontiers in Molecular Neuroscience* 12 (2020), https://doi.org/10.3389/fnmol.2019.00334.

for learning."[307] Yet when used wisely, it is a powerful tool to cement learning.

* * *

We see emotion prominent in Jesus' life and experience. He felt a full range of human emotion but never allowed emotions to lead Him to sin. He identified with other's pain, as reflected in the shortest verse in the Bible. When He learned that His friend Lazarus had died, John writes, "Jesus wept" (John 11:35)." After He rose from the dead, he joined two strangers on their way to a village called Emmaus (Luke 24). They didn't recognize Him until right before He disappeared. After they realized who they had been with, they talked about how Jesus had stirred their emotions. "Were not our hearts burning within us while he talked with us on the road and opened the Scriptures to us?" (Luke 24:32) Jesus even used negative emotions. He often angered the religious elite and hypocrites in His day, and He evoked guilt in Peter after he denied Jesus.

Jesus not only challenged the thought processes of His learners but their emotions as well. "He nurtured the emotional life as well as the intellectual life of His disciples."[308] He would rebuke some emotions, like anger when the disciples wanted to call down fire from heaven on the Samaritans when they didn't welcome Jesus (Luke 9:54). He would model emotions like grief (mentioned above when Lazarus died), compassion for others (what He felt for those who were shepherd-less (Matt. 9:36), and joy when the disciples returned safe and

---

[307] Daniel T. Willingham, *Why Don't Students Like School?*, p. 57.
[308] Walter Albion Squires, *The Pedagogy of Jesus in The Twilight of To-Day*, First Edition (George H. Doran, 1927), p. 137.

reported success from the preaching tour He sent them on (Luke 10:21).

Jesus understood how emotion moved people's behavior. He seemed to follow a general pattern in His teaching. He would arouse His learners thinking, and alongside this stage, there was "development of the appropriate emotional attitudes."[309] Then would come the practical application of His teaching to be seen in changes in their conduct—the doing of what He said. He sought to tap the deep inner springs of action (emotion and attitude) which would lead to actual action. Jesus followers "learned to feel deeply and purposefully quite as truly as they learned to think deeply and accurately."[310] As He instructed and appealed to emotion, right decisions become more certain.

True followers of Jesus aren't merely academic theorists or impractical emotionalists. Rather, as our emotion links with right thinking, we can change the world. As you craft and deliver your talks, start them on a positive note, look at ways to increase positive emotions throughout your talk, and acknowledge your own negative emotions before you deliver your talk. When you acknowledge and label your negative emotions, you decrease their intensity, freeing up more cognitive resources to communicate more effectively.[311]

* * *

---

[309] Squires, *The Pedagogy of Jesus in The Twilight of To-Day*, p. 156.

[310] Squires, p. 162.

[311] Matthew D. Lieberman, *Social: Why Our Brains Are Wired to Connect* (Crown, 2013), Kindle e-book loc. 3123.

PRACTICE TWO: LIMIT COGNITIVE DISSONANCE

In the 1950s, psychologist Leon Festinger proposed the theory of cognitive dissonance.[312] The theory suggests that our minds are designed to hold attitudes, beliefs, and behavior in harmony. When they aren't, we feel an uncomfortable sense of dissonance and respond in one of three ways: we change our current belief to fit the new information, we seek to find new evidence to confirm our current belief which we prefer, or we simply disconfirm or ignore the new evidence. Educator Piget calls this "cognitive dissonance disequilibrium," when ideas conflict with what a person already has in their schema (those neural manila folders).[313]

When we behave in ways inconsistent with our attitudes, our attitudes tend to change in the direction of our behavior. Research shows that people shift their attitudes to rationalize or justify their behavior.[314] Because cognitive dissonance feels uncomfortable, we adjust our attitudes to reduce the discomfort.

Fear prompts this move to allay the discomfort. God created us to explore the world yet also keep ourselves safe. However, sometimes we confuse safety with comfort, and we can get hooked on comfort. Harvard Medical School professor Dr. Susan David describes it this way, "If something feels comfortable—as in familiar, accessible, and coherent—our brains signal that we're just fine where we are, thank you very

---

[312] "Cognitive Dissonance Theory | Simply Psychology," accessed July 3, 2020, https://www.simplypsychology.org/cognitive-dissonance.html.

[313] Constance Kamii, "The Equilibration of Cognitive Structures: The Central Problem of Intellectual Development. Jean Piaget, Terrance Brown, Kishore Julian Thampy," *American Journal of Education* 94, no. 4 (August 1, 1986): 574–77, https://doi.org/10.1086/443876.

[314] James Crimmins, *7 Secrets of Persuasion: Leading-Edge Neuromarketing Techniques to Influence Anyone*, 1 edition (Wayne, NJ: Weiser, 2016), p. 74.

much. And if something feels new, difficult, or even slightly incoherent, fear kicks in. And while fear comes in all shapes and sizes, and sometimes it appears in disguise (as procrastination, perfection, shutting down, unassertiveness, or excuses), it speaks only one word: no, as in 'No, I'll just screw it up.' 'Nah, I won't know anyone there.' 'Nope, that will look awful on me.' 'Nuh-uh, thanks; I'll sit this one out.'"[315]

When you give a talk, you hope to evoke change in your learners. Every potential changed behavior will evoke some degree of cognitive dissonance as well as fear or anxiety. Uncomfortable or unfamiliar ideas make us feel, well, uncomfortable. The key lies in not creating too much cognitive dissonance. As a communicator, you want to avoid being so far ahead of your learners and so contradictory to their beliefs that they immediately shut you out.

On the other hand, we must sufficiently challenge them which will create some internal discomfort. Some new knowledge will inevitably seem counter-intuitive, difficult to embrace, or troublesome to the learner. Perhaps, as researchers Meyer and Land suggest, knowledge should be troublesome, and teachers should be troublemakers.[316] Learning requires challenge to existing beliefs, but our challenge should not be so far removed from current beliefs that it evokes strong cognitive dissonance and resistance to learning.

Making the change seem accessible (how easily something is understood) can help motivate your learners to embrace your challenge. People naturally bias decisions toward the familiar. The more familiar (and understandable) something

---

[315] Susan David, *Emotional Agility: Get Unstuck, Embrace Change, and Thrive in Work and Life* (Avery, 2016), p. 166.

[316] Meyer, J.H.F., "Threshold Concepts: Troublesome Characteristic," accessed May 31, 2020, https://www.ee.ucl.ac.uk/~mflanaga/popupTroublesomeness. html.

seems, the more we judge those things as less risky or less difficult, and thus we become more likely to embrace them.

One study[317] asked participants to read instructions for a routine. One group received the instructions in an easy-to-read font. The other group received the same instructions in a font that took more effort to read. The researchers then asked each participant to estimate how much time it would take them to complete the described routine. Those with the accessible font estimated it would take eight minutes. The group with the more difficult-to-read font estimated it would take twice as long.

So, making things seem more accessible makes them seem easier to do. In your talk, make the change you suggest seem accessible and doable without creating too much cognitive dissonance. The disequilibrium that cognitive dissonance creates is a powerful motivator when rightly used. Jesus created this dissonance in Peter when He taught the parable of the weeds. Peter then asked Jesus to explain it (Matt. 15:15). When Jesus talked about the difficulty of rich people entering the Kingdom (Mark 10), He created dissonance in His disciple which in turn evoked this question from them, "Who then can be saved?" The dissonance He created in their minds stirred their curiosity to resolve the dissonance.

* * *

PRACTICE THREE: LEAD WITH WELL-PLACED STORIES

In a prior chapter, I suggested that a story can pique the interest in your listener. Not only will stories do that, but they can enhance learning in general because they leave both

---

[317] David, *Emotional Agility,* p. 167.

physical and emotional traces in the brain as they evoke the neurotransmitter called oxytocin.[318] Jesus masterfully used stories. We call His stories parables[319]—earthly stories with heavenly or spiritual meanings. He'd start with the people's understanding of earthly matters and then use what they knew to explain spiritual matters.[320] He took His followers to the next step by bridging the natural to the spiritual.

The word parable, from the Greek word *parabole,* means analogy or comparison. The Hebrew word for parable is *mashal,* and rabbinical teaching incorporated over 1,000 parables to interpret the Torah. Parables fall into one of three categories: illustrations that help listeners grasp a concept, those that conceal a concept, and those that draw a parallel between a fictional story and reality. A third of Jesus' recorded teachings consisted of parables (30-60, depending on how you count them).

Parables generally included a two-part structure—the narrative itself and the explanation which put it into context. Most parables included six parts, following the general pattern storylines use today:[321]

1. A general introduction to build anticipation about what comes next—Jesus would often begin His parables with, "The Kingdom of God is like ... "

---

[318] Paul J. Zak, "Why Inspiring Stories Make Us React: The Neuroscience of Narrative," *Cerebrum: The Dana Forum on Brain Science* 2015 (February 2, 2015), https://www.ncbi.nlm.nih.gov/pmc/articles/PMC4445577/.

[319] "Rabbinical Methods of Instruction," accessed December 26, 2019, http://healing2thenations.net/papers/rabbinical.htm.

[320] Wasukundi.

[321] "Rabbinical Methods of Instruction."

2. The introduction of the characters in the parable—For example, Jesus began the parable of the Prodigal son with, "A man had two sons ... "
3. The plot to help readers identify with the story
4. The conflict which focuses on the problem needing a solution
5. The resolution that connects to real life (some parables ended with no resolution, leaving it to the listener to resolve it)
6. And finally, the call for the listener to decide or make application to life

Jesus used these comparisons from daily life or nature to illuminate many spiritual truths. Parables assume that what is valid in one sphere (daily life) is also valid in the other (spiritual). His parables invited His audience into "participation and involvement."[322] His stories weren't stories simply for the sake of storytelling. Rather, He wanted His learners to think about and heed the truth behind the story.

The disciples even noticed how often Jesus used them, as this question from them illustrates, "Why do you speak to them in parables (Matt. 13:10)?" He used story to open conversations (John 1:38; 8:10), prepare people for instruction (Matt. 17:25), get them to reflect (Matt. 20:22), probe for motives (Matt. 22:18), and even answer questions (Matt. 21:23-24).

* * *

---

[322] "What Can We Learn from Luther the Preacher?," *ChristianityToday.Com*, November 11, 1983, https://www.christianitytoday.com/ct/1983/november-11/what-can-we-learn-from-luther-preacher.html.

Storytelling is deeply rooted in history, dating to 4000 B.C. in Egypt. It provided a way to remember stuff for people in oral cultures without the ability to write. Memory in these ancient cultures was quite accurate because they used emotion when they told stories.[323] Researchers have actually discovered that storytelling goes as far back as 27,000 years ago when cave paintings were drawn. Those same researchers noted in a review of research on stories, "Memory is memory for stories, and the major processes of memory are the creation, storage, and retrieval of stories."[324]

Storytelling was a way for people to understand each other more effectively in contrast to using generalizations and abstractions. One study noted, "The teller and the listener come together on a cognitive and emotional level that allows the listener to relate to the teller from his or her own personal framework and thus grasp the teller's perception of the content at the same time. This represents a remarkable, and yet very common, interpersonal experience."[325] In other words, story helps us get immersed in another's thoughts and feelings which command our attention.

Researchers in one fMRI study sought to find a measure of story comprehension. They noticed what they called a neural coupling between the teller of a story and the listener.[326] They wrote, "The greater the anticipatory speaker-listener coupling, the greater the understanding." Most studies prior to the date

---

[323] Craig Eilert Abrahamson, "Storytelling as a Pedagogical Tool in Higher Education," *Education* 118, no. 3 (Spring 1998): 440.

[324] R. Eric Landrum, Karen Brakke, and Maureen A. McCarthy, "The Pedagogical Power of Storytelling," *Scholarship of Teaching and Learning in Psychology*, August 15, 2019, https://doi.org/10.1037/stl0000152.

[325] Abrahamson, p. 441.

[326] Greg J. Stephens et al., "Speaker–Listener Neural Coupling Underlies Successful Communication," *Proceedings of the National Academy of Sciences of the United States of America* 107, no. 32 (2010): 14425–30.

of this study had not examined both a communicator and a listener. Their study examined the brains of both.

The study involved one person telling a story while in a fMRI machine and another listening to the recording of the story while they lay in another fMRI. The study discovered that similar parts of both the teller's brain and the listener's brain were activated, though there was a delay between the teller's brain and the listener's brain. The stronger the neural coupling, the greater the story comprehension.

Neural coupling means that a speaker's neurons and a listener's neurons fire in the same patterns. They overlap or sync, so to speak. The study found that emotions from a storyteller created empathy for the speaker in the listener. Many areas of the listener's brain light up in storytelling because the listener interprets the events as happening to themselves[327] as if it were a genuine experience, a process called mentalizing. Storytelling evokes emotion in the brain of the listener which helps cement learning.

Dr. Uri Hasson at Princeton University has also researched the power of story.[328] By using fMRI, he played a 50-minute film that told a story for volunteers. He recorded their brains' response patterns. The volunteers then audio recorded their own recollections of the film. He then played those recordings to another group of volunteers and recorded their brain activity while they were in an fMRI. Amazingly, the brain patterns of the original group who viewed the film matched the second group who only *listened* to the recordings the first group made. The power of their language alone evoked the same mental experiences as if they had watched the film.

---

[327] Landrum, Brakke, and McCarthy, "The Pedagogical Power of Storytelling."
[328] Anderson, pp. 18-19.

Similar research shows that by simply telling a story, you can "implant ideas, thoughts, and emotions into...listeners' brains."[329] Storytelling profoundly impacts learning because it activates many brain areas such as language, visual, sensory, and motor centers.[330] And when more of the brain gets used, learning deepens.

Good stories will create interest, help learners remember material better, make material accessible, and create a learner-communicator connection.[331] One researcher noted, "We remember things that are woven together with a plot, are meaningful to us, have a vivid impact on our mind, or made us feel—good or bad. We remember stories that stir our emotions." [332] Fundamentally, stories help learners personalize content, make it relevant, and thus deepen learning.

You could use a story in multiple ways:[333] to capture attention, incite surprise, connect to your listeners with personal anecdotes, associate it to the content, facilitate problem solving, communicate facts in a more accessible way, or present a problem or dilemma. Stories will help your learners connect the pieces during your talk and help keep those pieces connected.[334] Good stories are easy to comprehend and remember. Good ones leave room to make inferences that require some thinking, but not too much. And when

---

[329] Stephens et al., "Speaker–Listener Neural Coupling Underlies Successful Communication."

[330] Carmen Simon, *Impossible to Ignore,* Kindle e-book loc. 2295.

[331] Landrum, Brakke, and McCarthy, "The Pedagogical Power of Storytelling."

[332] Landrum, Brakke, and McCarthy.

[333] Gabriel McNett, "Using Stories to Facilitate Learning," *College Teaching* 64, no. 4 (October 2016): 184–93, https://doi.org/10.1080/87567555.2016.11 89389.

[334] Abrahamson, "Storytelling as a Pedagogical Tool in Higher Education."

learners think about a story's meaning, it means they want to remember which further imbeds learning.[335]

From a brain perspective, what makes them so powerful? Stories create memory networks that store information across many regions of the brain.[336] They include the feeling center, the motor center, the visual center, and the thinking center. Stories engage all parts of our brain because they touch on our actions, experiences, and feelings.[337] They create mental pictures, and since the brain remembers visual better than verbal, we retain more. And the more vivid a story, the greater the impact.

Stories can even downregulate our primary fear center (the amygdala) as they engage our frontal thinking centers, thus dampening negative emotions that can hinder learning.[338] And storytelling also increases the neurotransmitter oxytocin (the trust hormone)[339] which can increase your learner's trust in you.

Stories should include what are commonly called the 4Cs: causality (events relate to each other), conflict (Luke Skywalker must destroy the Death Star), complications (many of them in Star Wars), and characters (Luke and Princess Leia are interesting characters). [340] Pixar uses what is called a story spine for their movies that looks like this: *Once upon a time there was ___. Every day, ___. One day, ___. Because of*

---

[335] Willingham, *Why Don't Students Like School?*, p. 67-68.

[336] Cozolino, p. 21.

[337] Sousa, p. 164.

[338] Cozolino, p. 192.

[339] Thomas Baumgartner et al., "Oxytocin Shapes the Neural Circuitry of Trust and Trust Adaptation in Humans," *Neuron* 58, no. 4 (May 22, 2008): 639–50, https://doi.org/10.1016/j.neuron.2008.04.009.

[340] Simon, Kindle e-book loc. 2305.

that, ___. Because of that, ___. Until finally, ___. And ever since that day, ___.[341]

So, when you craft your stories, keep these questions in mind:

1. Does your story reflect a plot over a timeline?
2. Does your story relate to your audience?
3. Are you trying to paint a picture rather than simply telling facts? Visual processing is more brain efficient than factual processing, and vivid images are stickier.
4. If you must use an abstract term, can you use a picture or metaphor to describe it? However, steer away from overused metaphors and clichés.
5. How can you connect to your listeners' emotions? The brain gives preferential treatment to emotional memories. They are more quickly and deeply encoded and more easily retrieved.[342]
6. Can you use "dual coding" in your story, showing a picture and simple text about the picture at the same time? You'll recall that dual coding helps create two neural tracks, one verbal and other image based, which enhance memory.[343] Dr. Carmen Simon wrote, "A picture is memorable when it is easy to label, and text is memorable when it is easy to picture."[344]

---

[341] "The Story Spine: Pixar's 4th Rule of Storytelling," accessed July 3, 2020, https://www.aerogrammestudio.com/2013/03/22/the-story-spine-pixars-4th-rule-of-storytelling/.

[342] Tyng et al., "The Influences of Emotion on Learning and Memory."

[343] James M. Clark and Allan Paivio, "Dual Coding Theory and Education," *Educational Psychology Review* 3, no. 3 (September 1, 1991): 149–210, https://doi.org/10.1007/BF01320076.

[344] Simon, *Impossible to Ignore,* Kindle e-book loc. 2441.

Storytelling is not a panacea. It can be used too often and learners can see stories as entertainment or simply a break from content rather than a tool to deliver content, so use them wisely.

* * *

In summary, *Principle Six: Emotion … Engage the Heart* means to use communication techniques that connect with the emotions and heart of your learners. I suggested three ways to do this. First, leverage what you know about emotion and learning. Second, minimize cognitive dissonance that would hinder learning. Third, use well-placed stories to connect with the heart.

Principle Six: *Emotion … Engage the Heart*

How can you help your learners feel your message?

- o Leverage emotional learning.
- o Limit cognitive dissonance.
- o Lead with well-placed stories.

In the next chapter, we'll look at *Principle Seven: Mindset… Cultivate Confidence.*

* * *

APPLICATION

1. In your own words, define cognitive dissonance. How might you intentionally use it in your next talk?
2. How have you used story in your talks? Too much? Too little? To what degree do you need to use story more often?
3. Recall from memory why story from a brain perspective is so powerful.
4. How do you file good stories? Do you have a system that makes it easy to find them for a talk? If not, consider creating a system (manual or electronic) to keep great stories you hear.

Check out the website for downloadable tools at
www.charlesstone.com/TEDfreebies

10

Principle Seven: Mindset ... Cultivate Confidence

They may forget what you said, but they will never forget how you made them feel. —Anonymous

---

Chapter Big Idea: Principle Seven—*Mindset ... Cultivate Confidence* answers the question, *How can you help your learners believe they can do what you suggest from your talk?* Three key practices will help you apply this principle:

1. Avoid the big neuromyths.
2. Act with a contagious spirit.
3. Accelerate your learners' motivation.

I never excelled at sports, but I did at academics. As I reflect over my early school experiences, I don't remember any specific subjects, classes, or assignments. I do, however, recall teachers who cared for me and instilled confidence in me.

Mrs. Moore, my sixth-grade teacher, often affirmed my ability to create interesting science projects. Mrs. McKay, my seventh-grade teacher, smelled like Vicks VapoRub™ and was so old she had even taught my dad when he was a kid. She saw my potential and challenged me to perform at a high level. Mr. Gann, my eighth-grade algebra teacher, saw my potential and helped me excel in a class that included high school seniors. Mrs. Cox, my ninth-grade science teacher, believed in me and still keeps in touch through social media. Mr. Hampton, my eleventh-grade science teacher, energized my love for the sciences. And my pastor while I attended GA Tech profoundly impacted my decision to go into full-time ministry.

All of these communicators instilled confidence in me because they believed I could learn, excel, and achieve. You can probably recall influential teachers, pastors, and coaches as well. A communicator's content, delivery, and learning insights certainly make our talks more effective. But in this chapter, I'll focus more on the personal dimension—what we can do to create a confident mindset in our learners so they believe they have what it takes to learn from you and are motivated to do so.

* * *

PRACTICE ONE: AVOID THE BIG NEUROMYTHS

In general, what we believe influences behavior. Likewise, what we believe about communication, how the brain learns, and memory influences how we craft and deliver our talks. The popularity of neuroscience has led to the proliferation of "neuromyths"—commonly held *false* beliefs about how the brain works. Earlier in the book, I mentioned one neuromyth—*goldfish have longer attention spans than humans.*

Neuromyths have also influenced how we communicate and teach. One study found that when researchers presented teachers with 32 statements on the brain, "on average, teachers believed 49% of the neuromyths, particularly myths related to commercialized educational programs."[345]

These neuromyths prevail for many reasons. They make great sound bites and headlines. They make the neuroscience of learning seem easy. They offer unscrupulous businesses a way to make a quick buck through selling products based on shaky science. And although some neuromyths may have a basis in the lab, their findings don't translate into real life. Neuromyths can tempt us to make an application where none exists.

Neuromyth expert Dr. Tracey Tokuhama-Espinosa notes, "Neuromyths are negative influences on quality education because they create false barriers to learning."[346] In fact, her research has yielded 70 neuromyths.[347] In this section, I only mention a few that can negatively impact learning the most, and you'll want to avoid them.

Jesus often challenged those who held false views. He said several times, "You have heard that it has been said … *but* I say to all of you." His listeners believed myths and untruths that He sought to correct.

---

[345] Sanne Dekker et al., "Neuromyths in Education: Prevalence and Predictors of Misconceptions among Teachers," *Frontiers in Psychology* 3 (2012), https://doi.org/10.3389/fpsyg.2012.00429.

[346] Tracey Tokuhama-Espinosa, *Neuromyths: Debunking False Ideas About The Brain*, 1 edition (New York: W. W. Norton & Company, 2018), Kindle e-book loc. 435.

[347] Tokuhama-Espinosa, *Neuromyths,* Kindle e-book loc. 450.

Neuromyth One: Attention span in a lecture lasts only 10-15 minutes.

This neuromyth is based on a 1978 paper[348] that was not an original research paper on attention but a literature review on how the amount of note-taking declined after 10-15 minutes during a college classroom lecture. The authors concluded that note-taking declined not because attention waned but because lecture content dropped, and a decline in note-taking did not necessarily indicate a decline in attention.

Neuromyth Two: Some students are left-brained and some students are right-brained.

Although our brains include two hemispheres, it's incorrect to say that a person is right-brained or left-brained. Research does indicate that some functions and tasks use more resources from one side than the other (i.e., speech processes in most right-handed people tend to lie predominately in the left hemisphere). However, "just because some tasks require more resources from one hemisphere, [it] does not mean individuals differ in terms of their brains."[349] Our brains work in a much more distributed way than previously thought.

Neuromyth Three: We have multiple intelligences.

Howard Gardner popularized the concept of multiple intelligences in the 1980s.[350] He theorized that we possess eight distinct forms of intelligence in varying degrees: linguistic, logical-mathematical, visual-spatial, bodily-kinesthetic,

---

[348] Hartley and Davies, "Note-taking."

[349] Yana Weinstein, Megan Sumeracki, and Oliver Caviglioli, *Understanding How We Learn: A Visual Guide*, 1 edition (London; New York, NY: Routledge, 2018), p. 36.

[350] Howard Gardner, *Frames of Mind: The Theory of Multiple Intelligences*, 3 edition (Basic Books, 2011).

musical, interpersonal, intrapersonal, and naturalist. Although some studies may point to specific brain regions where these intelligences are found, many have criticized his theory for several reasons. His theory lacks large-scale studies. Many believe that his eight intelligences are simply different manifestations of general intelligence. Others have criticized his theory out of concern that teachers would base their teaching on a theory that is scientifically controversial.[351]

Educators and scientists, however, largely agree that a "general" intelligence exists, often called "g," which is mostly heritable. "G" might relate to how quickly the brain's neurons fire or to the capacity of working memory. In addition, having a lot of "g" predicts people will do well in school and the workplace.[352] It's not equivalent to IQ but rather represents a component of it.

Until a few decades ago, scientists thought intelligence was primarily fixed at birth and environment could only shift IQ a bit. But many studies have shown that average IQ has grown substantially in the last few decades which is now called the Flynn Effect after the person who first described it, James Flynn. This research shows environmental factors such as good nutrition and health care can affect IQ.[353] Both genetics and environment have cognitive consequences, as educational expert Daniel Willington writes, "Small differences in genetic inheritance can steer people to seek different experiences in their environments, and it is differences in these

---

[351] C. Branton Shearer and Jessica M. Karanian, "The Neuroscience of Intelligence: Empirical Support for the Theory of Multiple Intelligences?," *Trends in Neuroscience and Education* 6 (March 1, 2017): 211–23, https://doi.org/10.1016/j.tine.2017.02.002.

[352] Daniel T. Willingham, *Why Don't Students Like School?*, p. 172.

[353] James R. Flynn, "Reflections about Intelligence over 40 Years," *Intelligence* 70 (September 2018): 73–83, https://doi.org/10.1016/j.intell.2018.06.007.

environmental experiences, especially over the long term, that have large cognitive consequences."[354]

So, it's accurate to say that in some ways, we can improve intelligence. As a communicator, you can build confidence in your learners by helping them understand that their intelligence is not fixed, but they can grow it. They don't need to believe that because they must work harder than others, they are dumb. In fact, students who believe they can improve their intelligence get higher grades than those who believe intelligence is an immutable trait.[355] This idea relates to mindset discussed later.

Neuromyth Four: Everyone has a unique learning style of how they learn best.

Multiple intelligences parallel this view. The theory states that each of us has a certain learning style that helps us learn best, such as auditory, visual, or kinesthetic. The theory infers that communicators should tailor their teaching to their learners' specific styles. However, intuitive as it may feel, learning styles appear to be another popular neuromyth.[356]

Although we do differ in our visual and auditory memories,[357] "There is not yet solid scientific evidence to support the claim that tailoring instruction to match learning styles works."[358] One study reviewed the scientific literature on

[354] Willingham, *Why Don't Students Like School?*, p. 176.
[355] Willingham, p. 179.
[356] Harold Pashler et al., "Learning Styles: Concepts and Evidence," *Psychological Science in the Public Interest* 9, no. 3 (December 2008): 105–19, https://doi.org/10.1111/j.1539-6053.2009.01038.x.
[357] Willingham, p. 156.
[358] Dr Thad A Polk, *The Learning Brain*, The Great Courses (Chantilly, VA: The Great Courses, 2018), p. 71.

learning styles and found 71 different models.[359] These researchers found very little agreement among the 13 models they considered most influential. If learning styles were based in science, scientists should agree on them at a basic level, but they don't.

This divergence probably comes from how researchers determine a learning style. Most studies simply ask students what learning style they like or prefer, but liking does not mean effectiveness. It's probably wiser to call such styles *preferences* rather than innate cognitive categories. However, tailoring what is called a learning style to material more suited to that particular style does enhance learning.[360]

So, stay vigilant about neuromyths. Don't let them sneak into your mindset, your preparation, or your talks.

* * *

PRACTICE TWO: ACT WITH A CONTAGIOUS SPIRIT

Emotional Contagion

A type of neuron, called a "mirror" neuron, was discovered by accident in the 1960s by a group of scientists at the University of Parma in Italy. They had implanted a probe into the motor cortex of a monkey's brain to study motor movements. When the monkey reached for food, their monitoring device noted specific neurons fired. But they also discovered

---

[359] F J. Coffield et al., "Should We Be Using Learning Styles? What Research Has to Say to Practice," January 1, 2004.

[360] Josh Cuevas, "Is Learning Styles-Based Instruction Effective? A Comprehensive Analysis of Recent Research on Learning Styles," *Theory and Research in Education* 13 (October 6, 2015), https://doi.org/10.1177/1477878515606621.

those same neurons fired when the monkey simply *observed* the researchers reach for food. In other words, the monkey's brain reacted in the same way as if he had actually reached for the food. These neurons eventually got the name *mirror neurons,* and fMRI studies have discovered that we humans also have those neurons, even though there is still some controversy about them.

When we watch others feel an emotion or take purposeful action, mirror neurons activate just as if we are experiencing those emotions or actions. When someone smiles at us, we smile back. When we see someone grimace, we also grimace. When we see someone tear up, we feel like tearing up. When we see someone get a shot on a TV show, we often turn our heads to avoid feeling similar pain ourselves. Even a baby just a few hours old will stick their tongue out if their mother sticks hers out. Mirror neurons map experiences we see in others on our own nervous system. Psychologist Louis Cozolino writes how mirror neurons affect us, "While our motor networks practice what we see being done by others, our emotional networks resonate with what we see is being felt by others. This emotional resonance then becomes the core of empathy."[361] These neurons bridge the gap between sender and receiver across what is called the "social synapse."

Daniel Goleman, a neuroscientist who popularized emotional intelligence, gives further insight into mirror neurons, "Mirror neurons have particular importance in organizations, because leaders' emotions and actions prompt followers to mirror those feelings and deeds. The effects of activating neural circuitry in followers' brains can be very

---

[361] Cozolino, p. 146.

powerful."[362] This mirroring effect is also true for communicators and teachers.[363] In other words, your actions, demeanor, and emotions, both good and bad, are contagious and impact learning. It's called emotional contagion.[364] A communicator's (or even a group's) stress, anger, or fatigue can be felt by the listener through these mirror neuron systems,[365] even without their awareness. Positive emotions are also transmitted through these neuronal systems. In fact, when we show support to others through our actions and expressions, we stimulate the production of feel-good neurotransmitters.[366]

Teachers who convey more positive emotions like confidence, enthusiasm, and optimism teach better, and students work harder to learn.[367] They communicate more clearly, give more complete explanations, make more connections between the content and the real world, and teach with greater enthusiasm. And their positive emotions evoke similar positive emotions in students, regardless of teaching attributes. As a result, students learn better. Conversely, teachers who feel angry and anxious don't teach as well.[368]

---

[362] Daniel Goleman and Richard E. Boyatzis, "Social Intelligence and the Biology of Leadership," *Harvard Business Review*, September 1, 2008, https://hbr.org/2008/09/social-intelligence-and-the-biology-of-leadership.

[363] Cozolino, p. 148.

[364] Adam D. I. Kramer, Jamie E. Guillory, and Jeffrey T. Hancock, "Experimental Evidence of Massive-Scale Emotional Contagion through Social Networks," *Proceedings of the National Academy of Sciences* 111, no. 24 (June 17, 2014): 8788–90, https://doi.org/10.1073/pnas.1320040111.

[365] Cozolino, p. 147.

[366] Cozolino, p. 154.

[367] Sarah Rose Cavanagh, *The Spark of Learning: Energizing the College Classroom with the Science of Emotion*, 1st edition (Morgantown, West Virginia: West Virginia University Press, 2016), p. 45.

[368] Sarah Rose Cavanagh, *The Spark of Learning: Energizing the College Classroom with the Science of Emotion*, 1st edition (Morgantown, West Virginia: West Virginia University Press, 2016), p. 48-49.

Proverbs 16:15 illustrates this idea, "There's life in the light of the king's face. His favor is like a cloud that brings spring rain." When an ancient king smiled at a subject, it implied that his favor experienced by that person would refresh their spirit. So, the tone you set can ripple through your entire audience.

Jesus must have often conveyed a contagious spirit. When He told His disciples to follow Him, they caught His enthusiasm and immediately followed as Matthew recorded in Matthew 4:18-22, "As Jesus was walking beside the Sea of Galilee, he saw two brothers, Simon called Peter and his brother Andrew. They were casting a net into the lake, for they were fishermen. 'Come, follow me,' Jesus said, 'and I will make you fishers of men.' At once they left their nets and followed him. Going on from there, he saw two other brothers, James son of Zebedee and his brother John. They were in a boat with their father Zebedee, preparing their nets. Jesus called them, and immediately they left the boat and their father and followed him."

We see His passion and zeal for God's purposes just after His first miracle when He turned water into wine (John 2:1-11). We see His fervor when He kicked the moneychangers out of the temple after seeing them cheat the people (John 2:13-17). As His disciples watched this play out, what they saw in Jesus reminded them of a verse from Psalms which John recorded, "His disciples remembered that it is written: 'Zeal for your house will consume me'" (John 2:17). Jesus exuded passion about His message, others saw it, and many embraced and mirrored that same zeal in turn.

Teacher Efficacy

Researchers have extensively studied a concept called "teacher efficacy." Teacher efficacy means a teacher believes they have the competencies to teach well and believes their teaching will make a positive difference in their students. Healthy teacher efficacy is one of the strongest indicators that students will learn well.[369] In other words, if you as a communicator believe God has given you the skills to communicate well and you believe what you have to say can make a difference in your listener, your beliefs about yourself can enhance learning in others.

One of the most renowned psychologists Dr. Albert Bandura developed the theory of self-efficacy which gives the basis for teacher or communicator efficacy. He says we can strengthen our self (communicator) efficacy in four ways:[370]

1. Mastery experiences—dedicate effort to grow your communication skills.
2. Social modeling—choose models of other communicators who do it well and learn from them.
3. Social persuasion—experience verbal encouragement from others.
4. States of physiology—because emotions, moods, and physical states influence how we interpret experiences and we often interpret our performance negatively, we must not judge ourselves too harshly when a talk doesn't go so well.

So, if you believe God has given you communication gifts and a message to share, your learners will feel your beliefs, and they will learn better.

---

[369] Ranjini Mahinda JohnBull, "Professional Development Effects on Teacher Efficacy:," 2013, 29.
[370] "Albert Bandura: Self-Efficacy for Agentic Positive Psychology," PositivePsychology.com, July 28, 2016, https://positivepsychology.com/bandura-self-efficacy/.

* * *

PRACTICE THREE: ACCELERATE YOUR LISTENER'S PERSONAL MOTIVATION

Researchers have discovered that several factors unrelated to brain processes affect how well learners learn.[371] They include:

- A sense of belonging to the learning group (acceptance by the group and the communicator)
- Psychological safety
- Belief that they can grow in their abilities and competence
- Belief that they can succeed (self-efficacy)
- Clarity and relevance of the material
- Belief that what they are learning has value to them

In other words, mindsets matter for motivation (more on mindsets below). You as a communicator influence many mindsets that enhance motivation to learn.[372]

When your learner feels personally motivated, they learn better. Your unique communication setting and your listener's work and home environment will influence how much you can an influence personal motivation. Even so, you can improve motivation when you help them change their

---

[371] Farrington et al., *Teaching Adolescents To Become Learners The Role of Noncognitive Factors in Shaping School Performance.*

[372] Jay McTighe and Judy Willis, *Upgrade Your Teaching: Understanding by Design Meets Neuroscience* (Alexandria, Virginia: ASCD, 2019), Kindle e-book loc. 2433.

mindsets because mindsets are malleable.[373] Some core mindsets you can influence include:[374]

Self-Efficacy—Self-efficacy refers to a person's confidence in their ability to achieve a goal. They may have high self-efficacy but low ability or high ability and low self-efficacy. If they don't believe they are capable of learning, they won't be motivated to even try. If they do believe they are capable, research shows[375] they will continue to work toward their goals, even in the face of difficulty. Here's the key idea. When a learner feels confident they can learn, they learn better.

Salience or Perceived Value—This means that when a learner places high value on what they are learning, they believe it is important or valuable to them (salient). That perceived value will enhance their learning.[376] The more you help your learners value what you are communicating and the more you help them "own their learning, both the process and the outcomes,"[377] the better they will learn.

Perceived Control—Perceived control means a learner believes they are in control of how much they learn, in contrast to depending on forces outside their control. Several studies have found perceived control can substantially impact motivation to learn.[378] The key idea here is that when a learner believes they have control over their learning, they learn better.

---

[373] Camille A. Farrington et al., *Teaching Adolescents To Become Learners The Role of Noncognitive Factors in Shaping School Performance: A Critical Literature Review* (Chicago: Consortium On Chicago School Research, 2013), p. 38.

[374] Farrington et al.

[375] Polk, *The Learning Brain*, p. 181.

[376] Olga Solomontos-Kountouri, Michailina Siakalli, and Petros Yiallouros, "IS IT IMPORTANT TO KNOW STUDENTS' PERCEIVED VALUE OF MATHEMATICS?," *Mediterranean Journal for Research in Mathimatics Education* Vol. 12, (January 1, 2013): 23–37.

[377] Immordino-Yang, Damasio, and Gardner, p. 55..

[378] Polk, p. 182.

Fixed Versus Growth Mindset—Perceived control relates to a concept called *mindset,* studied extensively by Dr. Carol Dweck.[379] She distinguishes between two mindsets, growth and fixed. People with a fixed mindset believe their talents and abilities are fixed and unchangeable, which is similar to low-perceived control.

In contrast, those with a growth mindset believe their abilities are malleable and changeable, similar to high-perceived control. People with fixed mindsets typically care more about demonstrating their innate ability by performing well, whereas a person with a growth mindset typically cares more about improving and mastering some domain of learning. When learners believe intelligence is more a matter of effort rather than innate smartness, they put more effort in and learn better. Research shows a growth mindset does enhance learning for many.[380]

So, help your learners believe that their ability to learn and change rests more on their personal effort within their control rather than on their innate ability or raw intelligence. When they understand and believe this insight, learning, perseverance, and engagement improves.[381] In fact, your own mindset (remember emotional contagion) can affect how well you convey a growth mindset. Help your learners see the following things about mindset:

---

[379] Carol S. Dweck, *Mindset: The New Psychology of Success*, Reprint, Updated edition (New York: Ballantine Books, 2007).

[380] David Yeager and Carol Dweck, "Mindsets That Promote Resilience: When Students Believe That Personal Characteristics Can Be Developed," *Educational Psychologist* 47 (October 1, 2012), https://doi.org/10.1080/00461520.2012.722805.

[381] Carol S. Dweck, "The Perils and Promises of Praise," *Best of Educational Leadership* 65 (summer 2008): 34–39.

1. Failure is an important part of learning. It's an opportunity.
2. Learning comes when you embrace challenges.
3. Obstacles provide learning opportunities.
4. Effort trumps intelligence when it comes to learning.
5. Let the success of others inspire you to learn.

One final note about mindset—when you praise your learners, praise them on their effort ("you worked hard ... persisted ... made extra effort") rather than ability ("you're smart"). Learners who receive praise on effort believe they can change their intelligence.[382]

Personal Agency

Related to mindset and perceived control is personal agency—believing that you "can." The more your learner believes they can do what you suggest in your talk, learn from it, and become the person God wants them to become, the more their confidence increases.[383] If they don't believe they can or attribute a past failure or poor performance to their lack of ability, they tend to withhold effort when faced with a similar task.[384]

As a communicator, the more you convey your confidence that your learner can *do it*, the greater their confidence grows that they *can* do it. Our learners work up to or down to the

[382] Willingham, *Why Don't Students Like School?*, p. 181.
[383] Cheon-woo Han, "Change and Stability in Achievement Goals Based on Instructional Tasks of a College Classroom," *American Journal of Educational Research* 4, no. 14 (August 22, 2016): 999–1007, https://doi.org/10.12691/education-4-14-3.
[384] Carol S. Dweck, "Reflections on the Legacy of Attribution Theory," *Motivation Science* 4, no. 1 (March 2018): 17–18, https://doi.org/10.1037/mot0000095.

perceived expectations we have of them.[385] They will sense your unspoken beliefs. Even giving them some control over their learning (see above on perceived control) can improve their confidence and motivation to learn.[386]

Also, fear of failure can stifle learning. Fear makes the brain constantly monitor performance which eats up working memory needed for learning. As fear amps up our brain's fear center (the amygdala),[387] it decreases test scores,[388] and past failures often give rise to fear future failure.

After Jesus rose from the dead, He pulled Peter aside for a candid talk (John 21). He asked him three times if he loved Him. It was a difficult conversation for Peter as it must have evoked memories of when he denied Jesus three times, but He knew Peter would play an important role in the early church. He needed to give him the confidence that even with his failures and hurt, Jesus had confidence in him. That's why Jesus had this talk with Peter.

The prophet Isaiah referred to this idea when he used metaphors to describe how God will not further hurt us when we hurt, "A bruised reed he will not break, and a smoldering wick he will not snuff out (Isaiah 42:3). Oftentimes, our learners need encouragement and confidence from us that no matter their past experiences, failures, or current setting, they can become what God wants them to become.

---

[385] Cozolino, p. 155.

[386] Mariale M. Hardiman, *The Brain-Targeted Teaching Model for 21st-Century Schools*, 1 edition (Thousand Oaks, Calif: Corwin, 2012), kindle e-book loc. 1311.

[387] Hiroki Toyoda et al., "Interplay of Amygdala and Cingulate Plasticity in Emotional Fear," Review Article, Neural Plasticity, 2011, https://doi.org/10.1155/2011/813749.

[388] Brown, Roediger, and McDaniel, Kindle e-book loc. 1263.

A Friendly and Safe Learning Environment

Sometimes, you may have little control over the environment where you speak or teach, and we have little control over our listeners' home or work environment. Some may come from highly stressed environments, and chronic stress can hinder their ability to acquire, retain, and even recall information.[389] Among school kids, the number one reported emotion is anxiety.[390] If you can create a learning environment with little stress, you can enhance their learning for this reason. In a low-stress environment, you're helping their brains "integrate the bodily and emotional functions of the right hemisphere with the social and language-oriented functions of the left hemisphere."[391]

Here's an example of how I managed a stressful environment. I was once asked to do an overnight retreat for Christian leaders at a hotel. When I arrived, I realized they had not provided me with a lectern or a lapel mike. I had already planned to hold a projector clicker in one hand and advance my notes on my iPad with the other. Now I was forced to create a make-shift lectern by placing a notepad on an unwieldy music stand which looked very unprofessional. I also had to hold the mike in one hand while using the other hand to interchangeably "click" my slides forward with the clicker and advance my notes on my iPad.

---

[389] Marian Joëls et al., "Learning under Stress: How Does It Work?," *Trends in Cognitive Sciences* 10, no. 4 (April 2006): 152–58, https://doi.org/10.1016/j.tics.2006.02.002.

[390] Reinhard Pekrun et al., "Academic Emotions in Students' Self-Regulated Learning and Achievement: A Program of Qualitative and Quantitative Research," *Educational Psychologist* 37, no. 2 (June 1, 2002): 91–105, https://doi.org/10.1207/S15326985EP3702_4.

[391] Cozolino, p. 20.

It was quite awkward, and I initially felt quite stressed. But I chose to make the best of it and not allow my frustration to diminish the friendly tone I wanted to set. I didn't bring the stress I felt to my demeanor during my talks. Had I done so and had the pastors picked up on it, I would have hindered their learning.

A friendly environment not only involves the physical space context but also the tone of the environment you set for your learners. Your listeners will learn best if the environment feels warm, inviting, and safe to them. The content or substance of your talk (the cognitive factor) certainly matters, but so do these non-cognitive factors.[392]

Jesus masterfully used His environment to communicate the Gospel. He preached the Sermon on the Mount on the northwest shore of the Sea of Galilee, using the backdrop of the mount as a reflector so that the people could hear him. When He spoke about worry in Matthew 6, He referred to flowers that were probably on the hill and birds that probably flew past the crowd as He spoke. In Matthew 13, the crowds were so large He had to sit in a boat away from the shore so they could hear Him. The water served as another acoustical enhancement. And Jesus trained His disciples in a safe and loving community. He rooted their spiritual formation within that community. When we experience community and safety with others, we learn better.[393]

Consider these five ways to create an environment friendly for learning:[394]

---

[392] Farrington et al., *Teaching Adolescents To Become Learners The Role of Noncognitive Factors in Shaping School Performance.*
[393] Karen F. Osterman, "Students' Need for Belonging in the School Community," *Review of Educational Research* 70, no. 3 (2000): 323–67, https://doi.org/10.2307/1170786.
[394] Farrington et al, p. 10.

1. Community—Create a sense that everyone there belongs. When we feel we belong in a group, we learn better. [395]

2. Growth—Convey that with effort, your learners can learn and grow.

3. Confidence—Similar to number two, instill confidence that they can learn.

4. Reward—Explain how what they learn holds value for them.

5. Praise—Praise the group for specific effort and behavior rather than using generalizations ("Your answers to my questions today were excellent" versus a generic "You were a great group today").[396]

The learning environment you create profoundly affects learning.

* * *

In summary, *Principle Seven: Mindset ... Cultivate Confidence* means to consider how to build confidence in your learners so they believe they can change, learn, and grow. I suggested three ways to do this. First, avoid letting common neuromyths affect how you view your learners or how you communicate. Second, bring your best, enthusiastic self when you give your talk. Third, intentionally find ways to spur your learners' motivation.

---

[395] Osterman, "Students' Need for Belonging in the School Community."

[396] Claudia M. Mueller and Carol S. Dweck, "Praise for Intelligence Can Undermine Children's Motivation and Performance," *Journal of Personality and Social Psychology* 75, no. 1 (1998): 33–52, https://doi.org/10.1037/0022-3514.75.1.33.

Principle Seven: *Mindset ... Cultivate Confidence*

How can you help your learners believe they can do what you suggest from your talk?

o   Avoid the big neuromyths.
o   Act with a contagious spirit.
o   Accelerate your learners' motivation.

In the next chapter, we'll look at the final principle, *Principle Eight: Transfer... Stimulate Life Application.*

* * *

APPLICATION

1. Think of a teacher, pastor, or coach who inspired confidence in you. What did they do? How can you include those qualities into your talks?
2. Google "neuromyths" and see what other kinds of myths are prevalent. How can you avoid letting those impact your talks?
3. Define emotional contagion. How do mirror neurons influence it? How could you remind yourself as you begin a talk to bring a positive, contagious spirit to the stage or classroom?
4. This chapter included seven concepts to consider that could accelerate your listeners' personal motivation. Review them and pick one or two that you could incorporate into a future talk.

Check out the website for downloadable tools at
www.charlesstone.com/TEDfreebies

11

Principle Eight: Transfer ... Reinforce Life Application

Transfer is the basis of all creativity, problem solving, and the making of satisfying decisions. —Madeline Hunter

---

Chapter Big Idea: Principle Eight—*Transfer ... Reinforce Life Application* answers the question, *What do you want your learner to do in response to your talk?* Three key practices will help you apply this principle:

1. Clarify the *"Now what?"*
2. Create clear cues.
3. Count on the Holy Spirit to work.

I once attended a conference with over 6,000 attendees, many holding earned masters and doctoral degrees. The conference included large plenary sessions as well as over 100 breakout sessions. The plenary speakers were the best of the best, and their talks were meant to inspire us to serve Christ better.

However, I noticed some common threads in the breakout sessions. Although most of the session leaders held PhDs, they seemed to lack a basic understanding about how people learn or how to present so that information sticks. Some filled their slides with so many words that my working memory got so overloaded as I read them that I tuned out what the speaker was saying. Some used odd colors and funny movements on their slides (like spinning the words as they appeared on the screen) which further disrupted my ability to pay attention. Some inundated us with so much information that their main points got lost. Some sped through difficult material so fast that although I am a quick learner, I couldn't follow them. Again, these were really smart people with PhDs.

I left many of the sessions with little direction about what they wanted me to *do* with the information they presented. They had failed to consider a crucial component that completes the learning cycle—a concept called "transfer."

What Is Transfer?

Transfer is simply life application. It's helping your leaners take the content from your talk into their life settings so they can apply it to their lives, work, families, and ministries. "Transfer is what learning is all about [...]. It's the ability to extract the essence of a skill or a formula or word problem and apply it in another context, to another problem that may not look the same, at least superficially. If you've truly mastered a skill, you 'carry it with you,' so to speak."[397] For the Christian, it's ultimately translating knowledge about your subject, God,

---

[397] Carey, p.154.

and the Bible into transformed attitudes, actions, and dispositions. Real transformation results in an engaged life, but not simply from encoded information.

Knowledge alone is not our end goal. In fact, in early Jewish history, the memory masters, the *tannaim* (see Chapter 3), were criticized not for the memory abilities but for the fact that their knowledge went no further than mechanical repetition.[398]

Our ultimate goal is to effect change in conduct and character as well as belief and behavior. That means your learners can take what you gave them in one context (church service, training session, class, etc.) and transfer it to the appropriate life context (personal spiritual growth, business application, marriage, etc.). It's the "core of problem solving, creative thinking, and all other higher mental processes, inventions, and artistic products."[399] Every communicator should strive to help their learners transfer the content from their talks to daily life.

That's what Jesus did. He aimed for life transformation in His followers. In the story of the Good Samaritan in Luke 10, a lawyer quizzed Jesus about how to define a neighbor. Jesus responded by telling him the story and then saying, "Go and do likewise (like the Samaritan did)." Jesus wanted this man to understand that real faith, not simply knowledge about faith, resulted in changed behavior and heart.

When He used parables and posed questions about them, He wanted people to reflect on their answers and explore the meaning for themselves. He wanted them to make deeper

---

[398] Mr. Birger Gerhardsson and Mr. Jacob Neusner, *Memory and Manuscript with Tradition and Transmission in Early Christianity*, trans. Mr. Eric J. Sharpe, Revised edition (Grand Rapids, Mich: Livonia, Mich: Wm. B. Eerdmans-Lightning Source, 1998), p. 107.
[399] Sousa, p. 153.

connections to how the parable's truth might apply to themselves. His first concern was not how much they knew or even what they should be taught but rather what sort of person they were to become.[400]

In fact, He *expected* transfer of His teaching to life. He used a parable of a house built on sand versus rock to illustrate that those who put Jesus' words into action (the ones who build their lives on God as their Rock) were the true wise ones (Matt. 7:24-27). Simple cognitive understanding falls short of Jesus' desire for us and our learners. He said the truly blessed are the ones who *do* the Word of God (John 13:17). He "emphasized action more than knowledge and stressed long-term rather than immediate results."[401] Jesus was after real change. He wanted explicit teaching to create implicit understanding to lead to new habits of the heart.

James also emphasized that we must "do" our faith. He said we must not simply listen to the word (a sermon, a lesson, a class), but we must do what it says (James 1:22). The Apostle Paul emphasized this as well when he wrote, "Whatever you have learned or received or heard or seen in me—*put it into practice*" (Phil 4:9, italics mine).

Lasting transformation, however, does not happen overnight. Real transformation can be messy, risky, and emotional. One extensive study of adult learners discovered 10 phases in the transformative process required for learning.[402] The learner:

---

[400] Charles Earle Raven, "The Teaching Method of Jesus and That of To-Day," *International Review of Mission* 18, no. 1 (January 1929), p. 48.

[401] David Naugle, "Information or Transformation? The Pedagogy of Jesus the Master Teacher and Its Implications," 2004, https://www3.dbu.edu/naugle/pdf/FridaySymposiumSp04/Pedagogy_of_Jesus.pdf, p. 13.

[402] Mezirow and Taylor, p. 19.

1. Faces a disorienting dilemma.
2. Self-examines.
3. Critically assesses assumptions.
4. Recognizes the connection between their discontentment and the process of transformation.
5. Explores options for new roles, relationships, and action.
6. Plans a course of action.
7. Acquires new knowledge and skills to implement the plan.
8. Provisionally tries out new roles.
9. Builds competence and self-confidence in those new roles and relationships.
10. Reintegrates those new perspectives into their life.

So, transformation takes time, and we as communicators play a pivotal role in fostering it.

Several factors help us foster transfer of new learning—how well we learned the information originally, the strength of cues, the context, and how much we practice the new learning.[403] Also, it's a two-part process. First, transfer *during* learning—when in long-term memory, past knowledge gets combined with new information to create an updated version of the information. Secondly, transfer *of* learning occurs when our learners apply their new learning later in their life context.

* * *

---

[403] Willingham, *Why Don't Students Like School?*, p. 123.

PRACTICE ONE: CLARIFY THE "NOW WHAT?"

In seminary, my preaching professor explained that every sermon should answer three fundamental questions: *What?*, *So what?*, and, *Now what?* These questions universally apply to any talk, sermon, training session, or lesson. The *What?* question relates to the content of a talk. The *So what?* question relates to why the subject is important to the learner (personal salience). And the *Now what?* question relates to what you ask the listener to do to incorporate the truth into their lives.

Answering the *Now what?* question specifies how you hope your listener will put into action Practice One (clarify the big take-away) from Principle One (*Clarity … Begin with the End in Mind*). Practice One makes your big take-away actionable.

Behavior change often precedes attitude change. One way to jump start behavior change is to get your learner to commit to a new behavior (what you hope your talk will evoke). In fact, if you can get people to *say* to themselves that they will *do* something, it improves the chances they will actually do it.[404] Gaining commitment is easier than changing behavior, but once you gain commitment, the chance of changed behavior increases. So, in your talks, challenge your learners to commit to an action. It will increase the chances they'll do it.

Just as a you clarify the over-arching big idea for a talk, it's important to clarify the specific behavior you want your learners to start or stop in the days ahead. I've heard many talks and sermons in my life that lacked any direction about what to do with the information. Don't let that be true of your talk. Clearly write out the behavior(s) you hope will change and repeat them a few times during your talk. Don't assume

---

[404] James Crimmins, *7 Secrets of Persuasion: Leading-Edge Neuromarketing Techniques to Influence Anyone*, 1 edition (Wayne, NJ: Weiser, 2016), p. 78.

your learners will get it the first time you explain the actionable step. And if you get your learners to imagine themselves doing that behavior for 30 seconds, it further increases the likelihood they will do it.[405]

In an earlier chapter, I explained the *So what?* question which related to salience, the perceived value or importance of your topic to your learners. Assuming you've answered that well, transfer next involves supporting the *Now what?* question with cues—reminders that help jog your listener's memory in the future to help them remember to apply their learning.

* * *

PRACTICE TWO: CREATE CLEAR CUES

In one of Jesus' most famous sermons, the Sermon on the Mount, He taught about worry. As large crowds sat on the hillside, Jesus created some cues from nature. As He probably pointed to birds and flowers around them, He reminded the people that God took care of them and they didn't worry about food or clothing. He then reminded the people that if God took care of those small parts of nature, they could trust that God would take care of them, so they need not worry. Jesus picked these common items in nature so that when the people saw them again in the future, those items could cue them to recall Jesus' message about worry.

That's what a cue does. It makes our message portable by taking it into a future context. A well-designed cue can help your learner recall and act upon what you said in your talk in a different setting in the future because they have taken the message with them (portability). Cues are critical because

---

[405] Simon, Kindle e-book loc. 1058.

research tells us that 60-80 percent of memory problems relate to forgetting to act on a future intention.[406]

You'll recall the Ebbinghouse Forgetting Curve from Chapter 1. It states that the average person will forget 70 to 90 percent of what you say unless you incorporate evidence-based learning principles that we've seen in Jesus' teaching. If new learning survives beyond a few days, it's probably destined for long-term memory storage and will not deteriorate further.[407] Since our learners only act on what they remember and not what they forget, our goal is to help them remember it in the future. It's called prospective memory—remembering to do something at a future time.

You want your learners to do just that—remember to do something different at a future time. A memorable cue they see later or think about will prompt them to search their memory, recall what you suggested in your talk, and then act upon it. Cues can dramatically increase their ability to remember and act upon prior knowledge.[408] A cue helps the learner locate and retrieve information from long-term memory, similar to how the name written on the tab on a manila folder cues us to the content of that folder.

Cues give information to a key component of the brain involved in memory—the hippocampus—that instigates the retrieval process of a memory (the behavior you hope your talk will motivate your listener to do). A cue triggers the memory trace in the hippocampus that sends signals to the parts of the brain where memories from your talk are stored.

[406] Simon, Kindle e-book loc. 415.
[407] Sousa, p. 79.
[408] Endel Tulving and Zena Pearlstone, "Availability versus Accessibility of Information in Memory for Words," *Journal of Verbal Learning & Verbal Behavior* 5, no. 4 (1966): 381–91, https://doi.org/10.1016/S0022-5371(66)80048-8.

It "reinstates" the memory and "remembers" it, although not perfectly.[409]

Dr. Carmen Simon states that cues work through a three-stage cognitive process.[410] First, your learner must recognize the cue at retrieval. Second, once your learner recognizes the cue, they must be able to retrieve the associated action. Third, if the new behavior is rewarding enough, your learner must be able to shift their action from what they are currently doing to the new action. The cue must be distinctive enough to motivate them to interrupt what they are currently doing to perform the new action.

So, how can you develop cues that help your learners remember, say, Point B at a future time when what they took away from your message was Point A? Dr. Simon suggests, "Constantly ask at Point A [your talk]: Am I showing my audiences a cue that attracts attention in a similar way to what they will see on their own?"[411] The more connections in your learner's mind that cue evokes, the better the recall.

Consider the questions below as you create cues ...

How can you make your cues easy to remember, recall, and repeat (cognitive ease)? Persuasion expert Dr. James Crimmins writes, "What springs easily to mind, whether it is people, phrases, ideas, or products, will be more liked, more believed, and more influential in our behavior. Cognitive ease makes us receptive."[412] Try to make it either verbally fluent so it easily rolls of the tongue or visually distinctive so it stands out from the other information you're giving.

I still recall an ad many years ago that Taco Bell aired to promote an upcoming Godzilla movie. A chihuahua had set a

---

[409] This process is called cortical reinstatement.
[410] Simon, Kindle e-book loc. 1096.
[411] Simon, Kindle e-book loc. 882.
[412] Crimmins, p. 31.

trap with three tacos lying under a box that was held up by a stick which in turn attached to a rope that the chihuahua held in its mouth. He was saying, "Here, lizard, lizard," over and over to entice him into the trap. But after he got a glimpse of Godzilla's size, he dropped the rope and said, "I think I need a bigger box." That visual and verbal cue immediately made me think of Taco Bell, and it still does. Even thinking about it now makes me hungry for a taco. That is a memorable cue.

How have you connected your cues to what's important to your learners? The more your talk makes your desired behavior for them *their* desired behavior because it's important to them (salient), the greater the chance the cue will evoke future action. Help them anticipate how a future action can bring positive benefits. Anticipating a reward can help spike dopamine which motivates us to action. When we get a reward, it's satisfying, and what gets rewarded gets repeated.

How can you leverage context dependent memory cues? One theory of learning, context dependent memory (also called the reinstatement theory), says that we can more easily recall information if the recall location, the context, is similar to where we learned it. When you can recreate the same environment in which the original teaching occurred, it enhances memory because many memories tie back to the context. As one scientist noted, "Recall is better if the environment of the original learning is restated."[413] Police investigators often use this and bring eyewitnesses back to the scene of a crime or an accident. Cues in the original environment trigger memories otherwise irretrievable.

Several innovative studies illustrate this. In one such study, students more accurately recalled words they learned when

---

[413] Carey p. 49.

the same kind of music played in the background as when they originally learned the words.[414]

In one of the most famous studies, scuba divers memorized words while underwater. An hour later, researchers quizzed them on what they could recall. One group got tested while underwater, and the other group was tested on land. The divers who took the test underwater got 30 percent more correct than the ones on dry land.[415] Reinstatement of their context apparently created cues (bubbles in the water, fish swimming by, etc.) which resulted in better recall.

Of course, we want our listeners to apply what we suggest in our talks in real world settings. We don't expect them to return to a church building, classroom, or training venue to reinstate the context to get the cue. So, how can you use context dependent memory?

First, you could remind your learners to envision elements in the physical environment where you held you talk. This envisioning experience can help them recover the cue.

Second, it's helpful to simply know that the context in which something is learned can cue us to remember the content of what we learned in that same context. The more we know about how learning occurs in our brains, the better communicators we become.

Third, your context may allow you to go to the environment where you hope a cue will evoke action. Let's say you're training students to recognize poisonous plants. In that case, a field trip to the woods to look for and identify the plants would provide the perfect context to teach this.

---

[414] Carey, p. 48-51.

[415] D. R. Godden and A. D. Baddeley, "Context-Dependent Memory in Two Natural Environments: On Land and Underwater," *British Journal of Psychology* 66, no. 3 (1975): 325–31, https://doi.org/10.1111/j.2044-8295.1975.tb01468.x.

Fourth, a related theory, mood dependent learning theory (or state-dependent learning),[416] states that re-creating the same mood in which people originally learned something can help with cue recall. It's easier to recall sad memories when in a sad mood and happy memories when in a happy mood. So in your talk, consider pairing an emotion you create in your talk (see Chapter 9) with a cue that might evoke a similar emotion in a future context.

How can you connect the cue to a physical or emotional reward? Connect the changed behavior to a reward or benefit the new behavior will bring so that both the action and the reward come to mind at the same time. Several factors will influence that ultimate choice: the effort it takes to get a reward, the time delay until we get that reward, the risk we perceive to get the reward, and the social impact related to that reward.[417] Creating the cue to relate to an emotional reward can motivate your learner to perform the future behavior.

Crimmins notes, "When we focus on feeling, we not only translate a rational reward into an emotional reward, we also translate a delayed and uncertain reward into one that is more immediate and certain. This is critical because [...] actions that are good for us often have delayed and uncertain rewards."[418]

Here are some examples of cues ...

In one research study of Catholics who remembered more of the sermon, they were given a card with a prayer to pray

---

[416] S. A. Pearce et al., "Memory and Pain: Tests of Mood Congruity and State Dependent Learning in Experimentally Induced and Clinical Pain," *Pain* 43, no. 2 (November 1990): 187–93, https://doi.org/10.1016/0304-3959(90)91072-q.
[417] Simon, Kindle e-book loc. 3218.
[418] Crimmins, p. 135.

each day. This simple reminder helped deepen their memory of the sermon's main point.[419]

Sometimes, I've pre-printed business-sized cards with the points from my message. We hand these cards out at the end and encourage people to tape them on their dashboard or bathroom mirror as cues to recall the gist of the message.

The week following your talk, you could send a text to people who attended with a question related to the action you hoped your talk evoked.

Let's say you are teaching about how to communicate real love to the significant people in our lives. In your talk, you could tell a story about what a person did to help another feel truly loved. If you tell the story well, your listeners will feel emotions that love can evoke. Your *Now what?* challenge might be to ask your listeners to recall what they felt like while you told the story in the following week, and while they feel that same emotional warmth, they should communicate to that significant person how much they love them. In this case, the mood (a warm heart) has become a cue for the behavior, even though the physical context has changed.

* * *

PRACTICE THREE: COUNT ON THE HOLY SPIRIT TO WORK

For true formation and change to occur, it requires more than cool techniques to help the brain remember stuff. We often underestimate that a person's existing habits and reflexes

---

[419] Joseph and Thompson, "The Effect of Vividness on the Memorability and Persuasiveness of a Sermon: A Test of the Elaboration Likelihood Model," *Journal of Communication & Religion* 27, no. 2 (November 2004): 217–44."

can overwhelm intentions to change.[420] So, it takes more than good teaching, good intentions, and a strong will to change. It takes God's power. For the Christian communicator, the Holy Spirit plays a profound role in learning and transformation.

The Holy Spirit is the ultimate memory maker and memory retriever. To overcome ingrained habits and belief, your learners need a Power to fuel their intentions—the Holy Spirit. Therefore, we should strive to be a tool for the Spirit to use to effect transformation, not simply information dispensers.

The Apostle Paul clearly stated, however, that talk does not equate to spiritual power. He wrote, "For the kingdom of God is not a matter of talk but of power" (1 Cor. 4:20). The power is the power of God as the Holy Spirit transforms us and our listeners.

Jesus said that when He left the earth, He would send another One, "The Counselor, the Holy Spirit, whom the Father will send in my name, [who] will teach you all things and will remind you of everything I have said to you" (John 14:26). So, the Holy Spirit helps us and our listeners learn (*teach you all things*) and recall and remember those things (*remind you of everything I have said*). He plays a supernatural *cueing* role in day-to-day living. And the better cues we create, the better our talks will sync with the work of the Holy Spirit.

As we apply sound learning principles illustrated in the life of Jesus, we can trust His Spirit to do His work. While in college, I was part of a Christian organization that shared the Gospel with other students. Our leaders often repeated a saying that went something like this, "Do your best in the power of the Holy Spirit and leave the results to God." That truth can keep our job as communicators in perspective. We

---

[420] Simon, Kindle e-book loc. 238.

do our best to apply sound communication principles when we craft and deliver our talk and pray for change in our leaners. But ultimately, we must leave the results to God, believing His Spirit will work in ways we will never know about this side of heaven.

* * *

A Few Other Factors that Enhance Transfer

Three other factors can influence transfer. The first, grit,[421] conveys two concepts: the ability to stay focused on long-term goals and the ability to delay gratification in the short term (self-control). Psychologist and writer Dr. Angela Duckworth popularized the term "grit" to describe the quality in a person to go a little longer and try a little harder to achieve their goals. In her research and writing, she notes that passion and perseverance can predict the degree a person achieves long-term goals.[422] Grit and the chance for ultimate, lasting change will vary in your learners. Some will enthusiastically apply your talks to their lives and stick with their commitments. Others will not.

Self-control, the second factor influencing transfer, has been studied in the oft-repeated marshmallow test.[423] In this experiment, children were left in a room with a marshmallow. They were told if they waited to eat it, the researcher would come back in a few minutes and give them another marshmallow.

---

[421] Angela Duckworth, *Grit: The Power of Passion and Perseverance*, Reprint edition (Scribner, 2016).

[422] Duckworth.

[423] "Marshmallow Test Points to Biological Basis for Delayed Gratification," ScienceDaily, accessed July 9, 2020, https://www.sciencedaily.com/releases/2011/08/110831160220.htm.

So, delaying gratification would yield two marshmallows. Some kids found ways not to eat the marshmallow. Others quickly gobbled it up. The early researchers followed these children into adulthood and noted that self-control (seen in the ones who waited) correlated with positive factors later in life such as improved grades and success in work. Later research discovered that education and socio-economic standing also affected their self-control.[424]

Both grit and self-control strengthen perseverance, a key character component needed for lasting transfer. Jesus often spoke about perseverance through persecution and difficulty (Matt. 10:22; 24:13) as did the Apostle Paul. He wrote, "We also rejoice in our sufferings, because we know that suffering produces perseverance; perseverance, character; and character, hope. And hope does not disappoint us, because God has poured out his love into our hearts by the Holy Spirit, whom he has given us (Rom. 5:3-5)." Paul ties the work of the Holy Spirit to our ability to persevere.

A third tool that can enhance transfer is to ask your learners to teach someone else what they learned from your talk. It's a form of active learning[425] called the "explanation effect."[426] When you must explain something to another, it forces deep elaboration. Peter Drucker, considered the founder of modern

---

[424] Tyler W. Watts, Greg J. Duncan, and Haonan Quan, "Revisiting the Marshmallow Test: A Conceptual Replication Investigating Links Between Early Delay of Gratification and Later Outcomes," *Psychological Science* 29, no. 7 (July 1, 2018): 1159–77, https://doi.org/10.1177/0956797618761661.

[425] Michelene T. H. Chi and Ruth Wylie, "The ICAP Framework: Linking Cognitive Engagement to Active Learning Outcomes," *Educational Psychologist* 49, no. 4 (October 2, 2014): 219–43, https://doi.org/10.1080/00461520.2014.965823.

[426] Joseph Williams and Bob Rehder, "Why Does Explaining Help Learning? Insight from an Explanation Impairment Effect," *Proceedings of the 32nd Annual Conference of the Cognitive Science Society*, January 1, 2010.

management said, "No one learns as much about a subject as one who is forced to teach it."

* * *

So, in summary, *Principle Eight: Transfer ... Reinforce Life Application* means to clearly include application(s) for your learners in your talk. I suggested three ways to do this. First, clarify the, *Now what?* Second, create clear cues. Third, count on the Holy Spirit to work.

In the next chapter, we'll pull everything together into a final concluding chapter.

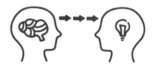

Principle Eight: *Transfer ... Reinforce Life Application*

What do you want your learner to do in response to your talk?

o Clarify the *Now what?*
o Create clear cues.
o Count on the Holy Spirit to work.

APPLICATION

1. Reflect on your most recent talks. How clear was your *Now what?* If it wasn't clear, how would you incorporate a clear *Now what?*
2. What kinds of cues do you regularly use to remind yourself to do certain tasks? What kinds work best for you? For your next talk, what is one cue you could build into it to help your learners apply the *Now what?*
3. How does the fact the Holy Spirit works in the hearts of believers give comfort to you after you have delivered a talk that may not have gone so well?

Check out the website for downloadable tools at
www.charlesstone.com/TEDfreebies

12

Conclusion

The truth will set you free. —Jesus Christ (John 8:32)

As you come to the final chapter, I hope you've been able to put a few more tools into your communicator's toolbox. The book has intersected the Master Teacher's communication principles with the latest in the neuroscience of learning. Eight core principles have resulted. The principles can apply to any setting, whether business, school, or ministry.

As you consider where you go from here to best apply what you've learned, I offer four final thoughts.

First, as you craft your speeches, lessons, training sessions, and sermons, let the eight questions guide their development. Take a moment to review them now:

1. *Where do you want to take your audience?*
2. *How can you get your audience to really listen to you?*
3. *Why should your audience listen (the "So what?" question)?*
4. *How can you beat the competition vying for the attention of your audience?*
5. *How can you help your audience feel your message?*
6. *How can you help your message stick in the minds and hearts of your audience better?*

7. *How can you help those in your audience believe they can change and do what you suggest?*

8. *What does your audience need to do after your speech, sermon, lesson, or training session?*

Second, apply the principles that work for you. Some will work more effectively than others, depending on your context. However, one general concept can work in every context. I referred to multimedia learning and how the brain's visual processing profoundly enhances learning. You can never go wrong by applying visual learning to your talks.

Try this simple experiment. I've included the "Healthy Learning Platter" below with the eight icons that represent the eight principles but without the corresponding words that summarize the principles. In your own words, see how many principles you can recall from memory by simply looking at the icons without looking at the answers I give you in the following paragraph.

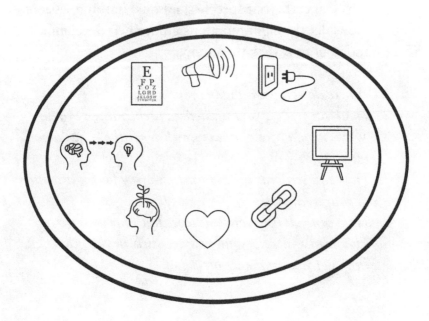

THE HEALTHY LEARNING PLATTER

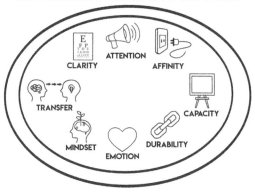

Here are the answers. The eye chart icon—Clarity ... Begin with the End in Mind. The megaphone icon—Attention ... Pique Interest. The plug icon—Affinity ... Create Connection. The chalkboard icon—Capacity ... Free Up Working Memory. The chain links icon—Durability ... Stimulate Long-Term Memory. The heart icon—Emotion ... Engage the Heart. The plant growing out of the mind icon—Mindset ... Cultivate Confidence. The two heads with arrows icon—Transfer ... Stimulate Life Application.

How did you do? You probably were able to recall the gist of many of the principles. That's the power of visual learning. Use it often.

Third, depending on your available preparation time, vary the degree you use the principles. As you create your talks, you could analyze them in-depth by using the checklist below, or you could simply use the "Healthy Learning Platter" as a high-level tool to jog your memory about the principles. You could also choose an in-between approach. Sometimes, you'll have enough preparation time to go in-depth using the checklist. Other times, you won't have enough time, and the "Healthy Learning Platter" will suffice. The more you apply these principles, the more intuitive they will become.

8 Core Communication Principles Checklist	Ideas
Principle 1: CLARITY - BEGIN WITH THE END IN MIND. ❑ Clarify the big take-away(s). ❑ Create a concept map. ❑ Capitalize on the primacy-recency principle.	
Principle 2: ATTENTION - PIQUE INTEREST. ❑ Adapt your material to the dynamics of attention. ❑ Add the appropriate attention grabber(s). ❑ Apply the concept of priming.	
Principle 3: AFFINITY - CREATE CONNECTION. ❑ Know your material. ❑ Know your audience. ❑ Help the audience know (and like) you.	
Principle 4: CAPACITY - FREE UP WORKING MEMORY. ❑ Maximize all the components of working memory. ❑ Minimize cognitive load. ❑ Marry new knowledge to prior knowledge.	
Principle 5: DURABILITY - STIMULATE LONG TERM MEMORY. ❑ Concentrate on enhancing recall. ❑ Choose sticky memory techniques. ❑ Create 'aha' moments.	
Principle 6: EMOTION - ENGAGE THE HEART. ❑ Leverage emotional learning. ❑ Limit the impact of cognitive dissonance. ❑ Lead with well-placed stories.	
Principle 7: MINDSET - CULTIVATE CONFIDENCE. ❑ Avoid the big neuromyths. ❑ Act with a contagious spirit. ❑ Accelerate learner motivation.	
Principle 8: TRANSFER - STIMULATE LIFE APPLICATION. ❑ Clarify the "Now What?" ❑ Create clear cues. ❑ Count on the work of the Holy Spirit.	

Finally, remember that some things are timeless, and some are not. The spoken word will always be with us. Speeches, sermons, lessons, and training sessions aren't going away, though the delivery technology may. The better we design and deliver them, the better our learners will benefit. However, the neuroscience of learning will constantly change. New tools that peer into the brain and faster computers to process that information will yield amazing new insight about how the brain learns, making some prior research obsolete.

On the other hand, though, the message and methods of Jesus never change. He nor His message will ever become obsolete. The writer of the book of Hebrews reminds us that, "Jesus Christ is the same yesterday, today, and forever" (Heb. 13:8). So, whether or not you are a follower of Jesus, I believe these principles will help you become a better communicator. I also believe that a personal relationship with Jesus connects us to a Power beyond our human resources that expands our communication's influence.

Much has changed in the last 100 years as scientists have discovered fresh insight about the brain and how it learns. Santiago Roman y Cajal (1852-1934), a Spanish surgeon and professor, is considered the founder of neuroscience. He earned a Nobel Prize for his study of the human nervous system, specifically the fundamental brain cell called the neuron. His research gave us a basic understanding about the nervous system upon which neuroscience has been built.

Of his many writings, one quote pointedly applies to us communicators, "Todo hombre puede ser, si se lo propone, escultor de su propio cerebro,"[427] which means, "Any man could, if he were so inclined, be the sculptor of his own brain."

As communicators, we must remember that we can profoundly influence how the brains of our learners get sculpted.

And as you communicate, may you be known as a wise, competent, and compelling "brain sculptor."

---

[427] Santiago Ramón y Cajal, *Advice for a Young Investigator*, trans. Neely Swanson and Larry W. Swanson, 1st edition (Cambridge, Mass: A Bradford Book, 1999), p. xv.

* * *

You'll find many free tools at the website at
www.charlesstone.com/TEDfreebies.
The tools include these and more:

o *Key Questions Communicators Must Ask*
o *Healthy Learning Platter*
o *8 Core Communication Principles Checklist*
o *Various visuals I used in the book*

Printed in the USA
CPSIA information can be obtained
at www.ICGtesting.com
LVHW041644070724
784834LV00002B/143